Which Dog Breed?

THE INSIDER'S GUIDE

LINDA WHITWAM

Table of Contents

1. Taking the Plunge

Apart from getting married or having a baby, getting a puppy is one of the most important, demanding, expensive and life-enriching decisions you will ever make.

Pick the right puppy, train and socialise him or her and you will have the perfect addition to your household. A living, loving member of the family who will love you unconditionally and who will be a joy to have around the house and to take out and about with you. What could be simpler?

Sadly, it doesn't always work out like that and many puppies end up in rescue shelters through no fault of their own. A leading figure in canine rescue says that the main reason dogs end up in shelters is "unrealistic expectations" on the part of the owner. In some other cases the dog stays with the family, but they are disappointed that he or she didn't turn out as they had hoped.

This book cuts through the hype and arms you with expert, inside knowledge of the 25 most popular breeds registered with the Kennel Clubs - and one that isn't. It also analyses the most popular crossbreeds and tells you what to look out for when buying one. Many new owners have no idea if they are buying a first, second or multi-generation cross – nor what implications that might have. This book demystifies the whole topic of F numbers with hybrid dogs.

If you suffer from allergies, you'll learn what dogs to consider and which ones are a complete no-go -and then it's up to you to spend time with the individual puppy before you commit.

The breeds are profiled with insight and you will read about the downsides of each one, as well as the highlights. This book will guide you beyond the countless pictures of gorgeous fluffy puppies to help you make a balanced decision on which breed or crossbreed would fit in best with you, your family, lifestyle and budget.

There is one factor above all others which plays a major role in people's decision on what puppy to get – and that is the look of the dog. Most people who are looking for a pet, rather than a working dog, choose a dog based on its appearance. And that is a big mistake. **Picking a puppy based solely on how it looks can be a recipe for disaster.**

That should only be a starting point. This book will help you to make a decision not just based on emotion or cuteness, but also on which puppy will be just right for you.

Getting a new living, breathing addition to your household who will live for 10 to 15 years is no small step and should not be taken lightly. Just like babies, puppies will love you unconditionally - but there is a price to pay. In return for their loyalty and devotion, you have to fulfil your part of the bargain. Here are some of the things you have to consider:

When you first bring your new puppy home, you have to devote several hours a day to his needs, which may mean taking time off work in the beginning. When he is little, you have to patiently teach your pup not to use your house as a toilet - like this Shar-Pei pictured! - then every day throughout his life you have to feed and exercise him.

If you want him to grow into a happy, well-adjusted adult dog you can take anywhere, you have to spend time socialising and training during his formative months. You also have to be prepared to part with hard cash for regular healthcare, and even more money in veterinary bills if he's ill.

If you are not prepared, or unable, to devote the time and money to a new arrival – or if everyone in your household is out at work all day – then now might not be the right time for you to consider getting a puppy. Dogs are faithful pack animals; they are entirely reliant upon us, their human companions, for their welfare and happiness. It may be fairer to a puppy to wait a while until you are in a position to give the time he needs.

Some people rush into getting a pup without thinking of the long-term commitment or what type of dog would best fit in with their lives. Once the seed of an idea to get a puppy is planted in your brain, it is hard to get it out and easy to get carried away emotionally by all the images of gorgeous fluffy little pups.

Getting a puppy is a long-term commitment. Before taking the plunge, ask yourself some questions:

Have I Got Enough Time?

In the first days after leaving his or her mother and littermates, your puppy will feel very lonely and maybe even a little afraid. You and your family have to spend time with your new arrival to make him feel safe and sound.

Ideally, for the first week - or preferably two - you will be around all of the time to help your puppy settle into his new home and start bonding with him. Book time off work in the beginning if necessary, but don't just get a puppy and leave him alone in the house a few days later.

You also have to spend time housetraining and obedience training. At one time it was thought that young dogs did not need training until they were adolescents. But canine behaviourists now stress the importance of the first four to five months of a puppy's life and how these formative weeks can influence the rest of his life. Start training as soon as he has settled into his new surroundings – usually within a week or two of bringing him home.

Although young puppies should not be over-exercised, it is still a good idea to get into the habit of taking them out of the house and yard for a short walk every day once it is safe to do so after the initial vaccinations.

Dogs have a natural migration instinct. This does not mean that they want to fly south for the winter, it means that they have a natural urge to move from one habitat to another – and daily walks fulfil this need. Allowing your dog to follow this natural instinct is a major key to keeping him happy, balanced and well behaved. New surroundings allow him to sniff and explore, they stimulate his interest, help him to burn off excess energy and help stop him from becoming bored and mischievous.

Your new arrival will need feeding daily, probably twice daily as an adult and several times a day with a young puppy – and in the beginning, food and drink does not stay inside a pup for long, so the result is a lot of tedious trips for you to the garden or yard.

How Long Can I Leave Him For?

This is a question we get asked all of the time on the website and one which causes a lot of debate among owners and prospective owners. All dogs are pack animals; their natural state is to be with others. Being alone is not normal for a dog, although many have to get used to it.

Another issue is the toilet. Dogs, especially puppies and young dogs, have far smaller bladders than humans, so leaving them unattended all day is not an option. Forget the emotional side of it, how would you like to be left for eight hours without being able to visit the bathroom?

So how many hours can you leave a dog alone for? Well, a useful guide comes from the rescue organisations. In the UK, they will not allow anybody to adopt if they are intending leaving the dog alone for more than four or five hours a day on a regular basis.

Dogs left at home alone all day become bored and, in the case of companion breeds which are highly dependent on human company for their happiness, often sad or depressed. Some of it will, of course, depend on the character and natural temperament of your dog. But a lonely dog may display signs of unhappiness by being destructive or displaying poor behaviour when you return home.

A puppy or fully-grown dog must NEVER be left shut in a crate all day. It is OK to leave a puppy or adult dog in a crate if he has been crate-trained and is happy there, but the door should never be closed for more than two or three hours during the day. A crate is a place where a puppy or adult dog should feel safe, not a prison.

Is My Home Suitable?

If you have decided to get a puppy, then choose a breed which will fit in with your living conditions. If you live in a small house or apartment, then a Great Dane would not be a good choice. If your house is full of expensive carpets and precious ornaments, then don't pick a high energy breed which will be lively indoors and also bring dirt and water into the house when returning from all the walks he'll need.

All dogs - even small ones, those with low energy levels and dogs living in apartments - need some daily time out of doors. If you live in a small flat on the 10th floor of a high rise block, then a medium or large dog, or small breed with high energy levels requiring lots of exercise, would not be a good choice.

Successful apartment living for canines involves having easy access to the outside and spending time housetraining. This may mean training the dog to use a pad or a tray as an indoor bathroom. If you can regularly take yours out at least three or four times a day to do what he needs to do, there is no need to indoor housetrain him.

If you live in a house and have a yard or garden, check that it is well fenced. When your puppy arrives, don't leave him unattended outside for long periods – he may dig, find a hole in the fence and wander off, bark his head off and annoy your neighbours, and with the price of pedigree dogs often over £1,000, or $1,500, he can also be a target for thieves. Brachycephalic (flat-faced) breeds such as the Bulldog, French Bulldog, Boston Terrier and Pug, can also overheat. Check there are no poisonous plants or chemicals he could eat or drink.

Inside, puppy-proofing your home is similar to baby-proofing. It involves moving anything breakable or chewable - including your shoes - out of reach of sharp little teeth. Make sure electrical cords and remote controls are out of the way – lift them off the floor if necessary. You may have to tie your kitchen cupboard doors together and remove any dangerous cleaning fluids or chemicals out of harm's way. Block off any off-limits areas of the house, such as upstairs or your bedroom, with a child gate or barrier - especially as he will probably be following you around the house for the first few days.

Family and Children

What about the other members of your household, do they all want the puppy as well? A pup will grow into a not-quite-as-cute adult dog which will become a part of your family for a decade or more. Are they prepared to share the workload of daily exercise and abide by the boundaries you set? For example, if you decide you don't want your puppy on the bed or furniture, will everyone stick to the rule?

Children will, of course, be delighted at the prospect of a playful little bundle of fur joining your family. If you do have children, choose one of the breeds or crossbreeds which is known to be good around youngsters. Some, particularly the companion breeds, seem to have a natural affinity or attraction to kids and babies.

Remind everyone that it's important your puppy gets enough time to sleep – which is most of the time in the beginning, so don't let enthusiastic kids constantly pester him. Sleep is very important to puppies, just as it is for babies. One of the reasons some young dogs end up in rescue centres is that the owners are unable to cope with the demands of small children AND a dog.

Remember that dogs are very hierarchical, in other words, there is a pecking order. Puppies will often regard children as being on their own

level, like a playmate, and so they might chase, jump and nip at them with sharp teeth. This is not aggression; this is normal play for puppies. Be sure to supervise play time and make sure the puppy doesn't get too boisterous; train him to be gentle with the children.

Older People

If you are older or have elderly relatives living with you, dogs can be great companions, provided they are not too boisterous. A larger breed, or one with high energy levels from working stock, such as a Border Collie, may be too much for a senior citizen. They may pull on the leash or be boisterous or destructive in the house (the dog, not the old person!) If you are older, make sure your energy levels are up to those of a young puppy. Ask yourself if you are fit enough to take your dog for at least one short walk every day.

Dogs can, however, be a real tonic for older people. My father is in his 80s, but takes his dog out walking for an hour every day – even in the rain or snow. It's good for him and it's good for the dog, helping to keep both of them fit and socialised. They get fresh air, exercise and the chance to communicate with other dogs and their humans.

Dogs are also great company at home – you're never alone when you've got a dog. Many older people get a puppy after losing a loved one (a husband, wife or previous much-loved dog). A dog gives them something to care for and love, as well as a constant companion. Sometimes a well-behaved adult dog may be a better option as housetraining and daily obedience training are not involved. Whether old or young, a dog is not a cheap pet - especially if veterinary fees are involved - so it's a good idea to check that the finances will support this new addition to the home.

Single People

Many single adults own dogs, but if you live alone, having a puppy will require a lot of dedication from you. There will be nobody to share the tasks of daily care, exercise, grooming and training, so taking on a dog requires a huge commitment and a lot of your time if the dog is to have a decent life. If you are out of the house all day as well, it is not really fair to get a puppy, or even an adult dog. Left alone all day, they will feel isolated, bored and sad. However, if you work from home or close to home or are at home all day and you can spend considerable time with the puppy every day, then great!

Other Pets

If you already have other pets in your household, spend time to introduce them gradually to each other. If you have other dogs, supervised sessions from an early age will help the dogs to get along and chances are they will become the best of friends. Some types of dog – such as Terriers and hunting dogs -have a natural instinct to chase and so may take more time to get used to having other small animals around. Some of these dogs have a high prey instinct and may never get used to living compatibly with other non-canines.

If you adopt an older dog and have other pets, make sure they get along before you commit, as not all mature dogs are able to change the habits of a lifetime if they have instinctively chased cats, for example. If you already have another dog, it is important to introduce the two on neutral territory, rather than in areas one pet deems as his own.

You don't want one dog to feel he has to protect his territory. Walking the dogs parallel to each other before heading home for the first time is a good idea to get them used to each other.

Cats can sometimes be more of a problem; most dogs' natural instinct is to chase a cat. An attention-loving puppy may see the cat as a threat and in a minority of cases it may take a long time (if ever) to accustom them to small pets.

A lot will depend on the temperament of the individual dog and at what age he is introduced to the other animal(s) – the earlier, the better. Your chances of success are greater if your cat is strong-willed and your dog is docile! If your cat is timid and your dog is alert, young and active, then your job will be more difficult.

Supervised sessions and patience are the answer. A pup may tease a cat, but in the end will probably learn to live with it. Make sure the cat does not attack the puppy.

Take the process slowly, if your cat is stressed and frightened he may decide to leave. Our feline friends are notorious for abandoning home because the food and facilities are better down the road. Until you know that they can get on together, don't leave them alone.

For a dog to get on with a cat, you are asking him to forget some of his natural instincts and to respond to your training. But it can be done successfully.

2. Types of Dogs

So now you have decided that you definitely want to get a puppy, the big question is **which type of puppy?**

Getting a pup is a huge commitment and not something to be rushed into. One thing that every prospective owner should keep in the back of their mind is this: an ugly puppy has yet to be born. All puppies are incredibly appealing, some are wrinkly, others are furry – but they are all without exception CUTE.

It is for this reason that we cannot recommend too highly the following course of action: Decide on what type of dog you want BEFORE you visit any litters. Once you see the little darlings, your heart rules your head and it is extremely difficult to walk away without agreeing to buy one - even if it's not the sort of dog you originally intended to get.

A dog is not a sparkly necklace, nor a fast car nor status symbol. It is a living, breathing creature with its own character, emotions and a lifespan of a decade or more and should not be bought on impulse. These Beagle puppies (pictured above) could well live for a dozen years or more.

According to a major figure in canine rescue, the main reason for dogs ending up in shelters is "unrealistic expectations" on the part of the owners. You may have an idealised image in your mind of snuggling up with your faithful companion, or wonderful walks through the countryside with Man's Best Friend. These images may come true, but the reality is that there is a lot of effort to be put in before you reach that stage.

Firstly, in finding the right kind of dog and secondly, in nurturing and training him so he becomes the dog of your dreams. For example, these Beagle pups require obedience training to teach them to listen to your commands, rather than to follow their natural instinct and wander off after a scent at the drop of a hat. This requires time, commitment and consistency.

I believe that there is a simple formula to maximise the chances of everything working out between you and your dog and the two of you having a happy life together.

Six Golden Rules

1. Do your homework before you buy a puppy. Take the time to research breeds, crossbreeds and mixed breeds before deciding on the type of dog that would best fit in with your lifestyle, finances and time commitments and energy levels.

2. Find a good breeder - one who is preferably recommended by your country's Kennel Club or the relevant breed society in your region. He or she will breed not only breed for looks and colour but, most importantly, for health and temperament. If necessary, wait until a suitable pup becomes available. DON'T be tempted by adverts on listings websites such as eBay, gumtree or nextdaypets. DON'T buy a cheap imported pup, or so called "rare colours", they don't exist. If you are buying a pedigree dog, it is either bred to breed standards or it is not. For "rare colour" read "colour not accepted by the Kennel Clubs or breed societies."

3. When your puppy arrives, take time off work or your other normal routines if necessary to be at home with him for the first week or, better still, two or more to help him settle in and overcome his fears.

4. Spend time every day obedience training your puppy for the first few months of his life – even if it is only five minutes a day - then reinforce it periodically throughout his adult life. This should include teaching him to walk nicely on the lead; especially important with large breeds, which will grow into powerful adults and the way you will control them then will be by using your voice, not brute force.

5. Socialise your dog. There is a critical window in a dog's life when he is aged between eight weeks and 18 to 20 weeks. How you treat him and what he is exposed to during this period will have a bearing on how he reacts to everything for the rest of his life. In safe conditions, introduce him to new people, places, other dogs and small animals, loud noises, traffic and different situations. Don't limit your time with him to the home and garden, take him out and about with you.

Exercise your dog every single day away from the home – no matter how small he is. Every dog has a natural instinct to migrate.

The Kennel Clubs class dogs in different breed groups according to what they have originally been bred for. Here we will list each group and its characteristics, along with the most popular dogs in that group and their typical traits.

To say that all dogs of the same breed group are alike would be akin to saying that all Americans are optimistic and friendly and all Brits are polite and reserved. It is, of course, a huge generalisation. There are grumpy, unfriendly Americans and rude in-your-face Brits. However, it is also true to say that being friendly and optimistic are general American traits, as is being polite in Britain.

It's the same in the canine world. Each individual dog has his or her unique character, but there are certain traits which are common within the different breeds and breeds in the same groups may also share certain similarities of temperament.

Pedigree, or purebred dogs, as they are known in North America, are bred to a **breed standard.** This is a blueprint for not only how each breed of dog should look, but also how it moves and – what a lot of people don't realise - what sort of temperament it should have. The breed standard is laid down by the main breed society in each country, and the Kennel Clubs keep the register of pedigree dogs. The dogs entered in conformation shows run under Kennel Club rules are judged against this ideal list of attributes, and breeders approved by the Kennel Clubs agree to breed puppies to the breed standards.

If you like a particular breed, you might be tempted to go for a less expensive puppy advertised by a non-approved breeder on a website or local newspaper and offered for sale without official Kennel Club registration documents. This is often false economy, as there is no guarantee that the puppy's dam and sire (parents) have been screened for any hereditary health issues which affect the breed. You also have little idea of the temperament of the parents.

Breed Groups

The breed groups are slightly different in the UK and USA and some dogs are listed in different groups.

The Miniature Schnauzer, for example, is listed in the Utility Group in the UK and in the Terrier Group by the American Kennel Club. As the owner of one, I have to agree with Americans. On our walks, Max (pictured) likes nothing better than chasing cats, squirrels, birds and anything else smaller than himself – a typical Terrier trait.

Gundogs – As the name suggests, gundogs were bred to work alongside men (and women) with guns. They all hunt by scent and can be divided into three types: the Pointers and Setters, which find the prey; the Spaniels, which flush game out of cover; and the Retrievers, which were bred to fetch game - often out of water - and deliver it to their masters.

These dogs are all medium to large in size, are generally good natured, playful and love to carry or fetch things. They have been bred to work and are usually fairly easy to train. They are also energetic, having been bred to perform a task, and often have a lot of stamina. A Spaniel or Retriever bred from working stock will require more exercise than one bred from show stock. Working dogs have the stamina to run all day, so if you like these breeds but your exercise time is limited to an hour or so a day, go for a dog from show (or conformation) stock. Pointers have high energy levels and some can have a nervous disposition.

Hounds – there are two types: scent hounds and sight hounds, and both were bred for hunting and are generally friendly. The sight hounds are the sleek speed merchants like the Greyhound, Whippet and Saluki. They are often gentle dogs, but can sometimes be aloof. They like chasing small creatures and are not always the easiest dog to train.

The scent hounds, like the Beagle, Basset Hound and Bloodhound, track prey using their incredible sense of smell. They are generally amiable and tolerant, good with families, but can wander off. All hounds are more independent and less reliant on human company than companion dogs.

Pastoral – this includes the herding dogs, such as all the Collies. Typically they are highly intelligent and sensitive dogs, sometimes protective, and require a great deal of exercise as they have been bred to do a full day's work. They can be trained to a high level and need plenty of stimulation to stop them becoming bored.

The other type of pastoral are the thick-coated dogs which were bred to guard livestock, rather than herd it. These large, strong dogs, like the Old English Sheepdog, and the striking Komondor, have strong protective instincts and are not always suitable for the first-time owner.

Terrier – these date back to ancient times and were originally bred to keep down vermin. The name comes from the Latin, Terra, meaning earth. They are feisty, having been bred to be extremely brave and tough, and to pursue fox, badger, rat and otter and other animals.

Today there are many different types of Terrier, but typical traits are that they are very alert and excitable, with strong characters. They have strong predatory instincts and chase small birds and animals. They can bark a lot and some have a tendency to be quick to snap if not socialised.

Toy – these breeds are small companion or lap dogs. Many were bred specifically to be companions, others have been placed into this category simply due to their small size. Trained well, they have sweet, friendly personalities, many can be quite vocal. They love attention and thrive on human companionship; some can be prone to separation anxiety. Toy breeds generally do not need a large amount of exercise. Some can be finicky eaters. They should be treated like dogs, not babies, as they can become spoilt, snappy and end up ruling the household.

Some, like the Miniature Pinscher and the French Bulldog, have been bred down from bigger dogs and may retain some traces of the characteristics of the larger breed.

Utility - This group consists of miscellaneous breeds of dog mainly of a non-sporting origin, including the Bulldog, Dalmatian (pictured), Akita and Poodle. The name Utility essentially means fitness for a purpose and this group consists of an extremely mixed and varied bunch, most breeds having been selectively bred to perform a specific function not included in the sporting and working categories.

Individual breed characteristics vary, according to what task the breed was originally bred to perform. This group is similar to the Non-Sporting Group in the USA, which also includes the Boston Terrier, Bichon Frise, Chow Chow and Shar-Pei.

Working - Over the centuries these dogs were selectively bred to become guards and search and rescue dogs. Arguably, the working group consists of some of the most heroic canines in the world, aiding humans in many walks of life, including the Boxer (pictured), Great Dane and St. Bernard. Generally these dogs are big, intelligent and protective and many are real specialists in their field who excel in their line of work.

As well as these breed groups, there are other groups or types of dogs with common characteristics. One such type is the **companion dog**. A canine which has been bred to be a companion to humans will generally require less exercise than working dogs, for example. They will be happy to spend time indoors close to you, and may even follow you around from room to room or nudge your hand indicating they want to be stroked.

These dogs like to be physically close to their owners and do not do well when separated from them for hours on end. They may be suitable for less physically active people or the elderly, but are generally not a good choice if you are out at work all day, when they will become lonely and depressed, leading to poor behaviour.

Time should be spent with a young companion puppy teaching him to be alone for short periods, gradually lengthening the time you are away from him. This will help to prevent separation anxiety, a common problem with companion dogs.

Another group of dogs are the brachycephalic breeds. These are short-faced dogs with wide heads. Breeding a foreshortened skull has led to some serious health problems, the most common issues being breathing, skin and eye problems, an intolerance to heat and even an elongated palate. This occurs when there is not room for all the soft tissue to fit inside the dog's head and which often requires surgery to help the dog breathe.

If you select a brachycephalic breed, be sure to select a puppy which breathes easily, and ask the breeder about the health records of the parents and grandparents - are they breathing effortlessly, have they undergone any corrective surgery?

The full list of brachycephalic breeds is: Affenpinscher, American Cocker Spaniel, American Pit Bull, American Staffordshire Terrier, Bichon Frise, Boston Terrier, Boxer, Brussels Griffon, Bulldog, Bull Mastiff, Cane Corso, Cavalier King Charles Spaniel, Chihuahua, Chow Chow, Dogo Argentino, Dogue de Bordeaux, English Mastiff, French Bulldog, Japanese Chin, King Charles Spaniel, Lhasa Apso, Maltese, Neapolitan Mastiff, Newfoundland, Pekingese, Presa Canario, Pug, Shar-Pei, Shih Tzu, Silky Terrier, Tibetan Spaniel, Valley Bulldog and Yorkshire Terrier.

The incidence of health issues varies between the brachycephalic breeds, generally the shorter the muzzle, the greater the problems. Three of the most popular breeds have well documented health issues: the (English) Bulldog, the Pug and the French Bulldog, although responsible breeders are taking steps to try and improve the health of these breeds. For example, the French Bulldog has moved from Category 3 to Category 2 in the Kennel Club's Breed Watch (see next section for details of Breed Watch).

Selecting the right breeder who breeds for health is especially important with brachycephalic dogs. It is also a very good idea to get your puppy insured from the day you take him home. Corrective surgery is expensive.

Another group is unofficially known as "the Bully breeds." These are breeds and crossbreeds descended from dogs originally bred to bait bulls, hence the name. The dogs share a common physical appearance of large jaws, stocky bodies and a short coat, and many are brachycephalic. They include any breed with the word "bull" in its name, as well as Mastiffs, Boxers, Rottweilers and Great Danes. By temperament they tend to be very loving with their owners, comical, some are protective and many have a stubborn streak, so patience is required when training.

Breed Watch

Before we look at specific breeds, it is worth remembering that, however expensive the puppy - and many pedigree puppies these days cost four-figure sums – this is only the starting point in terms of expense. As well as normal feeding, annual vaccinations, regular healthcare and grooming expenses, you will also incur hefty veterinary fees if your dog has a serious health problem.

Breeding for a particular physical feature or colour from a narrow gene pool has led to inherent health issues within many breeds. In recent years, the Kennel Club, breed societies and responsible individual breeders have been making strides to reduce some of these problems.

In 2014 the Kennel Club (UK) launched its **Breed Watch Fit For Purpose** campaign. It identified a number of breeds and designated them as Category Three on Breed Watch. Category Three is classed as: "High Profile Breeds - Breeds where some dogs have visible conditions or exaggerations that can cause pain or discomfort."

The following breeds are on the list: Basset Hound, Bloodhound, (English) Bulldog (pictured here), Chow Chow, Clumber Spaniel, Dogue de Bordeaux, German Shepherd (previous page), Mastiff, Neapolitan Mastiff, Pekingese, Pug, Shar-Pei, and Saint Bernard.

The KC states: "The Kennel Club works closely with the clubs for these breeds in identifying key issues to be addressed within the breed, obtaining the opinion of breed experts on the issues identified, advising on how breed clubs can effectively address health and conformational issues and investigating how the Kennel Club can assist."

The reason for listing these breeds is twofold. Firstly, so that you can follow this link: www.thekennelclub.org.uk/services/public/breed/watch then click on the breed you are interested in and view the points of concern. If you still decide that this is definitely the breed for you, then you can ask your chosen breeder what he or she is doing to address these health points with his or her puppies. The list for the Bulldog, for example, is:

❖ Hair loss or scarring from previous dermatitis
❖ Heavy overnose wrinkle (roll)
❖ Inverted tail
❖ Lack of tail
❖ Pinched nostrils
❖ Significantly overweight
❖ Sore eyes due to damage or poor eyelid conformation

❖ Tight tail
❖ Unsound movement

If you are picking a Bulldog puppy, choose one where these traits are not in evidence.

The second factor is cost. All pedigree dogs have a predisposition towards certain inherited conditions - some more than others. But if you choose a breed with hereditary health issues of concern, you are statistically more likely to incur veterinary bills at some point in the dog's life. Are you sure you can afford them – not to mention the heartache if your dog falls ill?

The American pet insurance company Trupanion lists these dogs as the most expensive when it comes to vets' bills (it does not take rare breeds into account), and it is interesting to note that most of them are regarded as "Bully breeds":

1. Bull Mastiff
2. Saint Bernard
3. English Mastiff
4. French Bulldog
5. Dogue de Bordeaux
6. Newfoundland
7. Cane Corso (pictured below)
8. Rottweiler
9. (English) Bulldog
10. Great Dane

One of the company's biggest payouts was for one of the smallest clients. Bruiser, a Chihuahua mix from Staten Island, NY, had cancer surgery and 22 rounds of radiation and chemotherapy, at a cost of $34,323.95!

The list of breeds in the less serious Category Two "Breeds with Breed Watch points of concern" are:

Afghan Hound, Bearded Collie, Bedlington Terrier, Borzoi, Bull Terrier, Bull Terrier (Miniature), Cesky Terrier, Chinese Crested, Collie (Rough and Smooth), Dachshund (Miniature Smooth-Haired), Dachshund (Miniature Wire-Haired), French Bulldog (this breed was previously in

Category Three and it is a tribute to breeders in the UK that they have reduced the health issues with this breed over the last few years), Gordon Setter, Irish Setter, Irish Wolfhound, Keeshond, Newfoundland, Norwich Terrier, Old English Sheepdog, Pomeranian, Pyrenean Mountain Dog, Retriever (Golden), Retriever (Labrador), Shetland Sheepdog, Siberian Husky, Sloughi, Spaniel (American Cocker), Spaniel (Clumber), Staffordshire Bull Terrier, West Highland White Terrier.

You may have set your heart on one of these breeds and the fact that they are on the list does not mean that you should not get one. But take a look at the points of concern and bear them in mind when selecting a puppy.

It is good advice for the owners of any puppy to take out pet insurance as soon as you get your pup home, don't wait until after a health problem has developed, you may find the insurance company will refuse to cover that particular issue.

By the way, all other breeds are listed in Category One, described by the Kennel Club as: "Breeds with no current points of concern reported."

3. Insider's Guide to the Breeds

This chapter looks at the pros and cons of the 25 most popular pedigree (purebred) breeds registered with the Kennel Clubs in the UK and USA and one breed that isn't registered, despite being a firm favourite.

This guide includes the breed's ranking according to canine psychologist Dr Stanley Coren's highly regarded Intelligence of Dogs List. The rankings were based on the dog's speed to obey commands, rather than instinctive intelligence. Some more independent-minded or stubborn breeds fared less well in the list, not because they didn't understand the

command, but because it took a lot of repetition before the dog chose to obey.

Bear in mind that a breed lower down the list may require more time and patience to train. The other side of the coin is that the breeds classed in the top two groups of 'Brightest Dogs' and 'Excellent Working Dogs' may require more exercise and mental stimulation to prevent them from becoming bored.

In 2008, the BBC aired the programme **Pedigree Dogs Exposed** which investigated canine health issues caused by the over-breeding of some purebred dogs. It caused a stir in the UK and around the world. Following this, The Kennel Club (UK) introduced Breed Watch, a list which serves as an 'early warning system' to identify points of concern for individual breeds.

Its purpose is to enable anyone involved in the world of dogs, especially show judges, to find out about any breed-specific conformation issues which may lead to health problems. These are known as 'points of concern'. Breed Watch also provides an excellent quick reference for prospective owners to check the health status of the breed they are considering. Breed Watch has three categories: Category 1 - this is the healthiest group with no current points of concern, Category 2 – 'Breeds with Breed Watch points of concern', and Category 3 (previously called

High Profile) 'for breeds where some dogs have visible conditions or exaggerations that can cause pain or discomfort'.

Major considerations when choosing a breeder should not just be how their dogs look, but very importantly, the health and temperaments of the puppies they produce. Ask about health certificates and any points of concern listed in Breed Watch.

A breed with several points of concern is statistically more likely to require more veterinary care than one with no major health issues listed. This guide to the breeds starts with the Labrador Retriever, the favourite in the UK and North America.

Labrador Retriever

Despite the rise in numbers of so-called "designer dogs", the Labrador continues to top the canine popularity list on both sides of the Atlantic, Australia and New Zealand - and by quite some margin. Classed in the Gundog Group by the Kennel Clubs, the Lab was originally bred to retrieve game and fish on shoots. But today the breed performs many different functions.

Labradors are large, adaptable dogs with easy-going and sunny personalities. They have solid temperaments and are not usually highly strung, like Terriers for example. They are generally loving, lovable and easy to train. Decide if you want a puppy from show (conformation) or working lines. Those bred from field, or working, lines are livelier, have more stamina and require more daily exercise.

Labradors have earned their place as the most popular family dog with a reputation for being good with children, as well as excelling in other areas. They are well known as Guide Dogs for the Blind, therapy and assistance dogs, and anyone who has ever seen one in action will marvel at their intelligence. The Labrador is listed as the seventh brightest in the Intelligence of Dogs list. This and their adaptable and generally easy-going personality make the Labrador a highly popular family pet.

There are three types of Labrador Retriever: yellow, black and chocolate, and opinion varies as to whether their temperaments vary slightly between the colours. The single biggest factor determining the temperament of any puppy is, however, the temperament of his or her parents. Try and see both, if possible.

Labradors need a lot of daily exercise – an hour and a half or more is ideal, split into separate walks. Dogs bred directly from working stock may need more exercise. Lack of exercise can lead to destructive behaviour or barking. Having been bred to retrieve from water, they have webbed toes and most love to swim. They also like to carry objects and chew, especially when young, so having a selection of toys and chews is a good idea. On walks, most love running after a ball or stick and fetching it back.

One of our dogs was attacked by a pack of five Labradors while trotting along a field last year and was lucky to escape with his life. This was a highly unusual incident as Labradors are not naturally predatory or aggressive, but all dogs need socialisation. It was a young, entire male Labrador which had not been properly socialised that triggered the attack and the other dogs then followed their natural pack instinct and joined the fray.

We did not blame the young dog for the attack, but his owner (who was extremely apologetic and paid all of the veterinary bills), firstly for not socialising the dog and secondly, for allowing five dogs to run free as a pack where there were lots of other dogs and people.

Labs have a double coat, a soft, downy undercoat and a harder guard coat help keep the dog warm and dry while swimming in cold waters. They shed twice a year and are not suitable for allergy sufferers. They do not need a lot of grooming, but should be brushed once a week to keep them clean and remove some of the loose hairs. They generally only need a bath if they are smelly – such as after rolling in something horrible (this was a popular pastime with our Labrador, Harvey).

According to Labs4Rescue, both sexes make good pets. In general, male Labradors are more dependent and females are somewhat more independent. For example, if you are at home working on your computer, your male Labrador will may well sleep under your feet, while your female may sleep in the next room and just come in and check on you periodically. Labs are also extremely greedy and eat anything put in front of them – and a lot that isn't! Monitoring the dog's weight and preventing obesity is a constant challenge for owners. However, extra weight puts extra strain on the dog's joints, and this is a common problem with middle-aged and senior Labradors.

There is some anecdotal evidence that Labradors bred from backyard breeders or puppy mills can be hyper, rather than having the normal, even temperament. (Backyard breeders are people with little or no knowledge of breeding dogs and are in it mostly for the money). Pick a breeder approved by the Kennel Club to avoid this.

The Lab is in Category 2 of Breed Watch. Points of concern are: "legs too short in proportion to depth of body and to length of back, and significantly overweight." Health questions to ask the breeder about are hip and elbow dysplasia, progressive retinal atrophy (PRA) and retinal dysplasia - both affect the eyes.

In the USA ask to see OFA (Orthopedic Foundation for Animals) certificates for hip dysplasia, and CERF (Canine Eye Registry Foundation) certificate for eyes. In the UK, it's BVA (British Veterinary Association) certificates. These are relatively inexpensive tests for breeders – in the UK around £50 to £60 (and OFA fees are often less than $50 per dog in the USA) – small price to pay considering the cost of a pedigree dog. Typical life expectancy is 10 to 12 years.

SUMMARY: Excellent, even tempered family dogs. Only commit to a Labrador Retriever if you can give him a good walk at least two or three times a day. Visit http://labs4rescue.com/faq.shtml for more information on the breed.

Cocker Spaniel

This is the second most popular breed in the UK, although less popular in North America, and is in the Gundog Group (Sporting Group in North America). The breed was originally called the 'Cocking Spaniel' as it was used to hunt Eurasian woodcock. When introduced to America, the breed standard was changed to make the dog more suitable for hunting American woodcock (this new breed became the slightly smaller American Cocker Spaniel).

The medium-sized Cocker is gentle and sporty with a happy-go-lucky temperament.

The breed is generally good with kids and makes a great family pet, provided you make the time to exercise and train him.

They are intelligent and optimistic and have a permanently wagging tail. They are also sociable dogs which don't like being left alone, being very loyal one-man dogs which form a strong bond with their owners.

If you buy a 'field' dog bred from working parents, be prepared for lots and lots of daily exercise, a

working Cocker has incredible stamina and is happy to run all day – and you still won't tire him out. Don't expect to keep him on a lead; Cockers love to run around with their heads down, sniffing in the undergrowth. For every mile you walk, an active Spaniel will run several more. His retrieving instincts may mean that from time to time he brings you gifts – even in the house, when you will be proudly presented with a shoe or a toy – with, of course, a wagging tail.

Show dogs are sturdier and heavier that those from working stock. Despite being a gundog, some Cockers are sensitive to loud bangs. They are 18th in the Intelligence of Dogs list in the 'Excellent Working Dogs' section.

Cockers make good family dogs, provided they get enough exercise. They are intelligent, eager to learn and easy to train – although some can have a stubborn streak. In this case, patience and persistence is required when training; Cockers are sensitive critters and do not respond well to shouting or harsh treatment. Some can be possessive, so you need to teach a Cocker games which involve him releasing his toy or other object. Due to their sensitivity, they also require early socialisation so that barking or poor behaviour does not develop.

The breed has a range of solid colours, including black, red, golden, liver (chocolate), black and tan, liver and tan, as well as bicolours, tricolours and roan (mottled). They are high maintenance on the grooming front, their long coats need daily brushing and/or cleaning and their long, furry ears are prone to infections, so they also need regular checking and cleaning. Many owners have their Cocker's coat trimmed by a groomer to prevent matting and keep the coat clean, so this is another expense to be considered. A trip to the groomer's will cost on average £20 to £30, around $30 to $50.

Cockers shed a lot and often have a doggy smell. They are not suitable for allergy sufferers and probably not a good choice for the very house-proud owner. Their coats gather dirt and lose large amounts of hair, and some Cockers (and Springers) can also display submissive urination, which means that they pee when excited or intimidated - wherever they are.

Cocker Spaniels are in Breed Watch Category 1, with no major points of concern. Health issues include ear infections and eye problems, such as progressive retinal atrophy (PRA), glaucoma and juvenile cataracts, as well as autoimmune disease and joint problems. Ask the breeder about hip and eye certificates. Life expectancy is 12 to 15 years, although the median age in a Kennel Club survey (UK) was 11 years and two months.

SUMMARY: Good family dogs. If you are looking at puppies, find out if they are from working or show lines and if you have less than an hour a day to exercise your dog, go for one from a show line. There is also some evidence concerning health and temperament issues with Cockers bred from unscrupulous breeders. Spend time to find a responsible breeder.

German Shepherd Dog

This versatile, athletic and fearless working dog has a large band of enthusiastic devotees and is quite possibly the most popular breed on the planet.

The German Shepherd Dog, as the name suggests, originated in Germany and is in the Pastoral Group in the UK and the Herding Group in the USA, having originally been bred as a herding sheepdog.

This breed has done just about every possible canine job: assisting the blind, sniffing out illegal drugs, apprehending criminals, serving in the armed forces and helping search and rescue teams, to name just some of the tasks he is capable of.

A loyal and devoted companion, the German Shepherd (which used to be called the Alsatian) is very affectionate with - and devoted to - his family. Many owners would say that this isn't a breed, but a lifestyle. This is undoubtedly an extremely rewarding dog for those who can give him the time he needs.

Energy levels vary from very high to more laid-back, but all German Shepherds need brisk walking every day and running free as often as possible. The breed is suitable for families who are prepared to put the required time in. It is also a good choice for fit outdoor enthusiasts. Puppy classes are highly recommended with this breed, in fact in our area there are puppy classes specifically for German Shepherd Dogs, where the pups and adolescent dogs learn to mix with other dogs and people and walk nicely on the lead without pulling.

The German Shepherd is a highly intelligent and physical breed which needs plenty of exercise and mental stimulation. The Shepherd loves and excels at every kind of canine activity, including agility, obedience, tracking and herding. It is third on Stanley Coren's Intelligence of Dogs list, behind the Border Collie and Poodle. Intelligence is defined as learning quickly and being able to excel at tasks, but this cleverness needs to be channelled. An intelligent dog can easily become bored.

Plenty of daily exercise and mental stimulation, such as training, games or agility, is the key to success with this breed. Early socialisation with other animals and humans is **essential**, as an under-socialised GSD can become over-protective, territorial and aggressive. Many bark a lot. It also has a strong tendency to chase and this should be channelled into games at an early age. The breed is not known for being overly-friendly with strangers, and generally makes a good guard dog.

There is a great deal of variation between the temperaments of different bloodlines of German Shepherds. When picking a puppy, find out what the parents were bred for and look at the temperament of both dam and sire; your pup will take after them. Again, there are reports of dogs with unwanted temperament traits being bred by disreputable breeders out to make money. Take time to find the right breeder and remember, the perfect German Shepherd results from a combination of the puppy you buy and the time you put in to training and socialising him; a combination of nature and nurture.

Here is a cautionary tale: an acquaintance had a lovely even-tempered GSD who used to calmly sit in the grassy lane outside their gate all day watching the world go by. We'd stroke her as we passed, and our dog would happily exchange sniffs with her. Bella passed away a few years ago and the owners got a new German Shepherd pup around a year later.

Silka has a completely different temperament to Bella. She is highly intelligent, bold and lively by nature and has not attended training or socialisation classes (neither did Jess). The owners have had to build a higher wall to keep her in the garden after she jumped out and bit the next-door neighbour; she barks constantly at people and other dogs; a post box has been built on the exterior garden wall to keep the postman safe; and she drags her owner around the village on a lead twice daily on her extremely short walks. Silka is very loving, but she has grown into a territorial and over-protective adult. With proper training and socialisation and enough exercise, she would have been a superb dog the owners could have taken anywhere.

Most German Shepherds are fine with other family pets if introduced when young. However, some are cat chasers, and many are dominant or aggressive with strange dogs of the same sex.

They have a thick, double coat which sheds constantly - their nickname is 'German Shedder' - making them entirely unsuitable for allergy sufferers. They require regular brushing, preferably outdoors, to remove some of the loose hairs and the occasional bath.

German Shepherds are in Category 3, the points of concern are: "cow hocks, excessive turn of stifle, nervous temperament, sickle hock and weak hindquarters." Health issues include hip and elbow dysplasia, which may lead to arthritis, degenerative myelopothy (like multiple sclerosis), von Willebrand's disease (a bleeding disorder) and heart issues. Ask the breeder about hip, elbow and eye certificates. Life expectancy is 10 to 13 years.

SUMMARY: The German Shepherd is highly intelligent and extremely eager to learn and work. The breed requires an owner with a high level of commitment to training and socialisation. His many talents may be wasted if all you are looking for is a family pet.

Golden Retriever

This is a large, friendly breed in the Gundog Group which originated in the Scottish Highlands in the late 1800s. It was bred to retrieve water fowl and upland game birds during hunting and shooting parties. Their soft mouths enabled the dogs to bring back the shot game undamaged.

Goldens are cheerful, easy to train and eager to please. They are patient with children, making them the perfect family dog – provided they get the time they need. They love everyone and get along well with new people and strange dogs. They are clever, being listed at number four in the Intelligence of Dogs, and can be trained to a high level.

The breed standard describes the temperament as: "kindly, friendly and confident" and it is this equable temperament which is the trademark feature of the breed. The Golden Retriever has adapted to so many roles that there is virtually nothing he hasn't done, except be a guard dog – a task for which his friendly temperament makes him quite unsuited – although he will bark to announce new arrivals.

He has been a guide dog, a drug and explosives detecting dog, a tracker and an obedience competitor. The breed has risen in popularity over the decades so that now it is often the largest entry at Championship Shows.

Goldens are energetic and loving and have an instinctive love of water and swimming. They need plenty of daily exercise – a couple of hours a day is ideal – as well as mental stimulation to prevent them from becoming destructive. A Golden who gets this is charming and a pleasure to be around. The good natured exuberance of young dogs should be channelled into exercise and activities.

They enjoy playing and fetching and are suitable as jogging or cycling companions. Like many breeds bred to carry things in their mouths, they love to chew - especially as puppies, so plenty of chews and toys is a good idea to help keep them occupied during their early months. Due to their size and energy levels, they are not suited to apartment life, being better suited to a large house and garden or yard.

The smooth, medium-haired double coat is easy to groom, and they only need a bath when smelly. This breed is regarded as an average shedder, but each individual hair is very long and you'll find them all around the house. This is definitely not a breed to be considered by allergy sufferers.

Golden Retrievers love their humans and do not do well when left alone for long periods, so they are not suitable if you are out at work all day. When they are lonely, they can become destructive. They are happiest in the midst of family life with plenty of physical and mental stimulation.

Goldens are listed in Breed Watch Category 2 with the following points of concern (the same as the Labrador Retriever): "Legs too short in proportion to depth of body and to length of back, and significantly. Some can be susceptible to cancers, as well as hip and elbow dysplasia. They can also suffer from epilepsy, ear infections, allergies, skin infections and hypothyroidism. Buying from a good breeder with a track record for healthy breeding stock and health screening will help to avert some of these problems.

Golden Retrievers love their food, and care has to be taken not to allow them to become obese. Typical lifespan is 10 to 12 years.

SUMMARY: A wonderful family dog if you're around a lot and have the time for a couple of hours' exercise a day.

Pug

The Pug is classed in the Toy Group by all the Kennel Clubs. Over the last decade the breed has enjoyed a big surge in popularity and is now in the top six on both sides of the Atlantic. The origins of the breed are uncertain, but it is thought they may even date back to before Christ.

The roots lie in Asia with the short-haired Pekingese, and some Shih Tzu along the way. Genetics suggest that the Pug's closest relatives today are two lesser known breeds, the Petit Brabancon and the Griffon Bruxellois.

The Pug's increasing popularity is due to a number of reasons. The breed is small, does not require a lot of exercise and is content with living in an apartment or small house.

He is also intelligent, spirited, playful, loving and loyal - and a Pug will make you laugh. To top it all he is also generally good with children and other animals and loves being part of a family.

The Latin phrase 'multum in parvo' - a lot in a little – is an often-used description of this small, muscular breed. So what's not to like with this entertaining little dog with the big personality?

Despite being intelligent, Pugs are only listed at 57th out of 110 in the Intelligence of Dogs. This is because they can be stubborn; if they don't want to do something, you have to pleasantly but firmly persuade them to do it - they do not respond well to shouting – and this is not always easy.

You have to be patient with training, make it fun, Pugs love games, as the breed can be a bit single minded if they sense they have the upper hand (or paw!) They are also not the quickest dogs to housetrain, so be prepared to be patient.

The Pug will adapt to you and your life; if you are lively and energetic, your Pug will be too; if you are a couch potato, your Pug will adopt this lifestyle. All Pugs love sleeping, but even couch potato dogs need daily walks. A Pug can be happy with 30 minutes or less of daily exercise, some get used to much more from an early age. They are usually fine with other people and dogs, provided they have been socialised.

Like all companion dogs, they love to be with their humans, and may follow you around the house, earning them the nickname 'shadow dog,' but they are not happy to be left alone for long periods.

A Pug has a short double coat which can be silver, apricot, fawn or black. They are light shedders, a weekly brush will do, but they are not suitable for allergy sufferers. You may also need to clean your Pug's facial wrinkles every week to keep them clean and prevent infections.

A Pug is one of the brachycephalic (flat faced) breeds, and many suffer from breathing problems. In some cases corrective surgery can be successful, but this is expensive. Snoring, snorting and snuffling are all fairly typical - they are also pretty windy at the other end too! They are sensitive to temperature and can have problems in too hot or too cool conditions.

Pugs are in Breed Watch Category 3. Points of concerns are: "Difficulty breathing, Excessive nasal folds, Excessively prominent eyes, Hair loss or scarring from previous dermatitis, Incomplete blink, Pinched nostrils, Significantly overweight, Signs of dermatitis in skin folds, Sore eyes due to damage or poor eyelid conformation and Unsound movement". Other health issues to ask a breeder about are hip and knee problems and a back condition known as hemivertebrae.

Check that the parents have been screened for these last problems. If a breeder says he or she doesn't need to screen because they have never had any problems, be wary. Obesity can become an issue with some Pugs. Lifespan is 12 to 14 years.

SUMMARY: If you are at home a lot and are looking for a small dog with plenty of character that does not need much exercise or grooming, then a Pug is worth considering. Make sure you buy a healthy puppy which breathes easily from an accredited breeder.

English Springer Spaniel

The English Springer Spaniel and Cocker Spaniel share a joint history and in the 1900s were born within the same litter. The smaller Cockers were used for hunting woodcock, while their larger littermates were used to flush - or 'spring' – game, startling the birds into the air to fly within the hunters' sights. In 1902 the Kennel Club recognised the English Springer as a separate breed.

The hardy Springer is the traditional rough shooting dog with great stamina capable of working all day. He's always ready to jump into water, even if it means breaking ice to do it.

As with the Cocker, the English Springer is in the Gundog Group in the UK and Sporting Group in the USA. Both have webbed feet. They are also used as sniffer dogs and you may see one in action at an airport.

Like the Cocker, the handsome English Springer has a very friendly, positive outlook on life, typified by his continuously wagging tail. His cheerful extrovert nature has endeared him to the general public, and he is in great demand as an energetic companion for a family – but only one which can devote many hours to exercising this lively dog.

In physical terms, the English Springer is bigger than the Cocker Spaniel with fewer coat colourings. The accepted colours are liver and white or black and white, or either of these with tan markings. The other main difference is in energy levels, although working Cockers also have high energy levels.

An English Springer has been bred to do a job and can run all day without getting tired. If you like the breed, but cannot devote a couple of hours a day to exercising one, take a look at a puppy from a show bloodline and check with the breeder how much exercise he will be happy with. If it still needs more time than you can give, consider a companion breed. Some owners say that English Springers can be more alert and 'needy' than Cocker Spaniels, which may have calmer dispositions, particularly those from show lines.

English Springers are lively and intelligent, ranking 13th out of 131 breeds in The Intelligence of Dogs List. If you don't want to hunt with your dog, you may decide to take part in agility, flyball, tracking or obedience. English Springers' lively, alert nature means that they like to be on the go and thrive on these activities. Their sunny dispositions also make them good therapy dogs.

These are people-orientated dogs and do not thrive when left alone. There are reports of some suffering from separation anxiety, leading to excessive barking, chewing or nervousness. They are more likely to be friendly with everybody, rather than one-person dogs. For this reason, they do not make good guard dogs, although most will bark if someone comes to the house.

They have a thick, high-maintenance coat which is weather resistant, but requires regular grooming. Like most Spaniels, the long, drooping ears are prone to infection and need regular cleaning and trimming.

With its love of the great outdoors and swimming and a long, shedding coat, this is not a breed recommended for allergy sufferers. Neither is it one for the house-proud, as Springers can get quite smelly when their coat gets wet or dirty.

Like all Spaniels, they can display submissive urination when excited or nervous. They do best with owners who give them constant structure when they know their place in the household.

The English Springer Spaniel is in Breed Watch Category 1 with no major points of concern. Health issues include hip dysplasia, ear infections and eye and skin problems. Ask the breeder about hip and eye certificates. Do your research and pick a responsible breeder, there are reports of dogs with unwanted temperament traits from unaccredited breeders.

SUMMARY: An energetic family companion who is happy as long as he gets enough exercise. Unless you're a hunter or enjoy several hours of outdoor activity a day, get a puppy bred from show (conformation) bloodlines.

French Bulldog

Small companion dogs have become increasingly popular over the last decade, and none more so than the French Bulldog. In the USA, the breed has become almost five times more popular over a 10-year span and it's a similar story in the UK.

Originally bred down from the larger (English) Bulldog, lace workers took this smaller version (which some say was bred with the Pug) to France in the late 1800s. The breed soon became popular, particularly among artists … and prostitutes! It was then reintroduced to England.

This distinctive-looking dog with the bat ears has been bred as a companion dog, and is classed in the Utility Group in the UK and Non-Sporting Group in the USA. Two of the reasons for the rise in popularity are his unique looks - you'll either love 'em or hate 'em – and the fact that a Frenchie does not need a lot of exercise or grooming. To cap it all, he has an easy-going personality, doesn't bark much and loves sleeping.

Frenchies have a mischievous streak, which has earned them the unusual nickname of 'The Clown in the Philosopher's Cloak'. This sense of fun can turn to stubbornness if they are not properly trained from an early age. They can become territorial and like being the centre of attention, which can lead to behavioural problems if they are overindulged.

They are ranked 58th - one behind the Pug - out of 131 breeds tested in The Intelligence of Dogs List. However, this is not because they are stupid, far from it, but rather that the tests were based on the speed of the dog to obey commands. A Frenchie may very well understand you, but all bull-type breeds have minds of their own. They will consider your command a request rather than blindly following it and a patient approach is required when training. The good news is that they really love their food, which is a powerful training aid with Frenchies.

Training is essential if you don't want your cute little Frenchie to rule the roost. Some are notoriously difficult to housetrain; starting housetraining as soon as you bring your puppy home and being extra vigilant for the first couple of weeks should help to prevent any problems.

The French Bulldog does not need much exercise, but should be taken for at least one walk a day of up to 30 minutes, some will be happier with more exercise if they get used to it from an early age.

They are stocky and compact with a short, low-maintenance coat. The occasional brush should suffice. However, they do shed and are not suitable for allergy suffers.

There is currently a big problem with "rare" colours. These are non-Kennel Club recognised colours bred by non-accredited breeders. Some of these so-called rare colours, such as "blue," fetch large amounts of money. These breeders are only breeding for a colour, not for health or temperament and owners are discovering many problems with these "rare" Frenchies. I personally know of two which have had to be put down (euthanized) due to temperament problems. At least one of them had been imported.

If you decide to get a Frenchie, DON'T buy a rare colour and don't buy an import. Many of these dogs have been kept in concrete sheds for weeks on end and not socialised, leading to problems later in life. Buy from a breeder accredited with the Kennel Club in your country. The only colour recognised for French Bulldogs are: brindle, pied or fawn (or white in the USA). Tan, mouse and grey or grey-blue are highly undesirable.

Frenchies are very affectionate dogs and, like all companion dogs, are not at all suitable if you are out at work all day. They are, however, suitable for older people or families, when it's best to introduce them to children and other animals from a young age, as some unsocialised French Bulldogs can be snappy towards other dogs. With their fine coats and tendency to overheat, they are predominantly indoor dogs and are suitable for people living in apartments.

The black and white ones may look similar to Boston Terriers, but the two breeds are very different. A Boston is much more alert and athletic, needs more exercise and has a Terrier's tendencies, whereas the Frenchie takes much more after the Bulldog in temperament and looks. Frenchies differ from Pugs in that they are physically less stocky and they have a more mischievous streak.

The French Bulldog is a brachycephalic (flat faced) breed, needs his face wrinkles cleaning and ears checking regularly, and may be susceptible to a number of genetic illnesses – another very important reason for picking a good breeder. In a list of the most expensive dog breeds based on claims paid out by the Trupanion Pet Insurance company (USA) since 2000, the French Bulldog was listed at number five. The company said: "The French bulldog was responsible for $384,000 in claims paid out. This breed is prone to allergies, and other respiratory problems."

The health of the breed is, however, improving with selective breeding of healthy stock by responsible breeders. Frenchies have moved from Category 3 to Category 2 in the Breed Watch List. Points of concern are: "Difficulty breathing, Exaggerated roach in the top line, Excessively prominent eyes, Hair loss or scarring from previous dermatitis, Incomplete blink, Incorrect bite, Inverted tail, Lack of tail, Overly short neck, Pinched nostrils, Screw tail, Signs of dermatitis in skin folds, and Tight tail."

Other potential hereditary health issues include spine and joint problems. Ask to see health certificates before committing to a puppy. Average lifespan is 11 to 14 years. Further useful information can be found in **The French Bulldog Handbook**, available on Amazon and Apple.

SUMMARY: An amusing companion dog suitable for somebody at home a lot. The downside is that many rack up big veterinary bills, mainly due to breathing problems. Only buy a healthy pup from a Kennel Club accredited breeder - whatever the cost, it should save you money in medical bills in the long run. Frenchies have a short, shedding coat. Some shed more than others and this is not a suitable breed for allergy sufferers.

Bulldog

One of the oldest breeds, the Bulldog - also called English Bulldog and British Bulldog - has gone from being in danger of extinction in the 19th century to making the list of top 10 most popular breeds on both sides of the Atlantic. Originally bred for the bloodthirsty entertainment of bull baiting, the breed suffered a massive decline when the sport was banned in 1832. A handful of enthusiasts began to breed the aggression out of the Bulldog to create a companion dog, with considerable success.

Today's Bulldog is one of the most instantly recognisable of all the breeds with his massive head and wrinkled face. Despite a fierce exterior, he is a

sheep in wolf's clothing, with a placid temperament and laid-back habits. No longer a sporting dog, he is classed in the Utility Group in the UK and Non-Sporting Group in the USA.

His nickname is Bully - or Sourmug - but nothing could be further from the truth.

It's true that Bulldogs have kept their stubborn streak, but they are generally the most placid of creatures, happy to snooze the day away next to - and even on top of - their owners. An adult Bulldog may weight 40lb to 55lb, but nobody has told him he's not a lapdog. He is known for his gentle nature, loves sleeping, and enjoys snuggling up on the couch or his owner's knee.

Despite his size, the modern Bulldog is a highly popular companion dog. He is predominantly an indoor dog and is suitable for life in a house or apartment, due to the fact that he does not need much exercise. A couple of short walks a day are usually enough. Like the Frenchie, he may show bursts of energy and dash round the house having a mad five minutes of play time, but does not have stamina.

He loves to be with people – so if you are out at work all day, don't get a Bulldog. Most Bulldogs like to chew if bored, especially when young. Go for a breed which is less dependent on humans for happiness. Bullies have big hearts and respond to anyone showing them kindness, rather than being one-person dogs.

They also have a reputation for being wonderful with babies and children. Many seem to have a natural affinity and protective instinct towards youngsters. However, a Bulldog is a powerful dog who doesn't always know his own strength, and young Bullies are often boisterous, so always supervise their time spent together.

Bulldogs are also very courageous. If properly socialised, they don't look to start a fight with other dogs – and usually get on well with other pets if introduced at an early age – but they will not back down if involved in a confrontation. Don't allow a Bulldog to get into a staring match with another dog.

Bulldogs are almost at the bottom of the Intelligence of Dogs list, with only the Basenji and Afghan Hound ranked lower. The breed's dismal showing is not due to the fact that the Bulldog doesn't understand the command, it's that he will weigh it up before deciding whether he wants to obey or not. Patience and persistence are required when training, but it must be done in an encouraging manner; Bulldogs do not respond at all well to shouting or physical violence.

This is one of the brachycephalic breeds and a recent survey by a large pet insurance company revealed that Bulldogs are one of the most expensive breeds in terms of healthcare. The trademark huge, flattened skull looks very appealing, but has led to some major health issues within the breed, and breathing problems are common. Many are unable to mate naturally.

Listed in Breed Watch Category 3, these are the points of concern for the Bulldog: "Excessive amounts of loose facial skin with conformational defects of the upper and/or lower eyelids, Hair loss or scarring from previous dermatitis, Heavy overnose wrinkle (roll), Inverted tail, Lack of tail, Pinched nostrils, Significantly overweight, Sore eyes due to damage or poor eyelid conformation, Tight tail and Unsound movement."

Although relatively undemanding dogs in terms of exercise and grooming, Bulldogs require care on an almost daily basis and are not recommended for first-time owners. Their facial wrinkles, ears and tails have to be kept clean to prevent infection, and they must not be left outdoors or exercised in hot weather as they are prone to overheating, which can be fatal.

In short, the Bulldog is the only dog for some dog lovers, and they can undoubtedly make extremely rewarding companions. Anyone thinking of getting one should first thoroughly research the breed and its sensitivities. Most importantly, choose an accredited breeder with a track record of producing healthy puppies. Don't just go for the looks, ask to see health certificates and check the pup's breathing. If he seems to be struggling for breath or wheezing, walk away - however cute he looks.

Typical lifespan is eight to 10 years, some may live slightly longer, although a UK survey revealed that the median lifespan of a Bulldog was a little over six years, taking into account those which died before reaching old age. **The Bulldog Handbook** http://amzn.to/1wRTrRS (or in the USA http://amzn.to/11BRBaC) is a good source of information on the breed and the specialist care required by owners.

SUMMARY: The Bulldog has a quiet dignity and a high pain threshold, so needs an attentive owner. One of the few larger dogs suited to apartment life as it has low exercise needs. Many potential health problems due to the extremely compressed face, so chose your breeder and then your puppy very carefully.

Beagle

The Beagle is consistently among the top five breeds in the USA and, although far lower down the list, the breed is becoming increasingly popular in the UK, according to Kennel Club statistics.

Dogs similar to the Beagle have existed for 2,400 years, with the modern breed having been developed in Britain in the 1800s. The origin of the name may lie in the French "be'geule," referring to the baying sound of the hounds when pursuing game, or possibly the diminutive size of the hound.

Belonging to the Hound Group, Beagles are scent hounds, originally bred to track hare, rabbit and other small game. Indeed, there are still packs of Beagles working today on both sides of the Atlantic, with their followers travelling on foot, rather than on horseback.

A Beagle has one of the best developed senses of smell of any breed, along with the Bloodhound and the Bassett Hound. This has led to the breed being employed as detection dogs around the world, sniffing out prohibited agricultural imports, foodstuffs and explosives. In the 1950s, two scientists began a 13-year study of canine behaviour. They tested the scenting abilities of various breeds by putting a mouse in a one-acre field and timing how long it took the dogs to find it. The Beagles found it in less than a minute.

They have a cheerful, gentle disposition and are even tempered. The breed is relatively healthy, listed in Breed Watch Category 1 with no major points of concern. One factor any prospective owner should be aware of is that the Beagle is a hardy, active dog which needs lots of daily exercise if he is not to become bored or destructive, particularly during the early years when he has higher energy levels. Many Beagles slow down as they grow older.

If you like the Beagle, but cannot give up a couple of hours a day to exercise him, you might want to take a look at a Puggle, a cross between a Beagle and a Pug. They have many features of the Beagle, but are slightly, less excitable and need less exercise. They also do well in cities, whereas a Beagle is happiest running off the lead in countryside.

By nature the Beagle is friendly and tolerant and, as an athletic working pack animal, is happiest with people and/or other dogs and plenty of exercise. Behaviour problems can develop if he spends too much time alone, when barking or trying to escape can become a problem. The main reason for Beagles being given up for rescue is their baying or barking.

Training and plenty of exercise is the best way of preventing yours becoming a problem barker. Beagles are intelligent but independently-minded, which is why they are ranked at 73 in the Intelligence of Dogs list, in the 'Lowest Degree of Working/Obedience Intelligence' section.

A typical scent hound, the Beagle is highly active and has a strong instinct for following a trail. He is happiest outside with his nose to the ground following a scent. This means that he is likely to forget you and wander off on his own if not supervised. He loves to run off the lead, but you need to make sure he is trained to return and keep a sharp eye on him. The Kennel Club says of the Beagle's natural desire to follow a trail: "This instinct is mimicked in his everyday behaviour in the park: the man with the lead in his hand and no dog in sight owns a Beagle."

The breed is relatively easy to train, although some dogs can be stubborn, and do best with an owner who combines kindness with firmness and clear leadership. They can be difficult to housetrain, and the correct use of a crate may help. Beagles generally get along well with children, provided they have been properly socialised around them and trained how to behave with them – the children as well as the dog. Youngsters should not tease a Beagle while he is eating or sleeping, and Beagles should be taught not to nip children when playing (they have a habit of 'mouthing' things when playing.)

The Beagle has a short, coat which is easy to keep clean, so doesn't need baths unless he has rolled in something horrible. Their short hair does shed, so they are not suitable for allergy sufferers. The most common coat is tricolour with a saddle, or patch of black, on the back, although any hound colour is acceptable. The drooping ears should be checked and cleaned regularly to prevent infections occurring.

There are two sizes of Beagle in the USA, one is 13" at the withers (shoulder) and the other is 14". In the UK, dogs can be anything from 13" to 16" tall. As with all breeds, males tend to be larger than females.

A relatively healthy breed, the Beagle is in Category 1 of the Kennel Club's Breed Watch, with "no points of concern". Health issues known to affect some Beagles include disk disease, epilepsy, dwarfism, hip dysplasia and immune disorders. There are no 100% health guarantees with any animal, but the best way of avoiding future health problems is to buy from an accredited breeder. Typical lifespan is 12 to 15 years.

SUMMARY: Easy going, gentle breed which needs regular exercise. May not be suitable for a household with cats or other small non-canine animals. With human leadership they make excellent pets, although they have tendency to wander off after a scent.

Border Terrier

The Border Terrier is extremely popular in the UK, although less so in the USA. Originally bred to hunt foxes and rats, the Border has shared ancestors with other Terriers, including Dandie Dinmonts, Patterdales and Bedlingtons.

He was bred to have legs long enough to keep up with horses and other foxhounds, and a body small enough to crawl into the burrows of foxes and chase them out. Although much older, the breed was officially recognised by The Kennel Club in 1920, and by the AKC in 1930.

The Border is a true Terrier, with their typical characteristics, and classed as such by all Kennel Clubs. The word 'Terrier' comes from the French *terre*, meaning earth, and also burrow. Most are lively and alert, and will chase small animals and birds at the drop of a hat. And as with all Terriers, the Border is full of character.

Border Terriers were bred to have the courage and stamina to work all day in all weathers. They were often left to find their own food and so have a strong hunting instinct which remains today.

They also have a powerful drive to dig and bark and have retained their high energy levels for a small dog. These traits can make the breed a challenge for some owners, while others find them to be wonderful companions who play hard and are extremely loyal and affectionate.

Temperaments and energy levels will vary according to bloodlines. If you want a less active Border Terrier, spend time choosing an accredited breeder who is not breeding from active working lines, and look at the temperament of the parents - or at least the mother, if the sire is not present. Is she feisty and noisy or more laid-back? Your pup will inherit his temperament from his parents.

Border Terriers need a lot of exercise for a small dog, a minimum of an hour a day is recommended, with a lot of this time spent running off the lead. But before you can do this, you have to train your dog to come back, as his hunting instinct will take him at breakneck speed out of your sight within minutes. The breed excels in hunting and hunting trails as well as agility and obedience contests.

One of the reasons for his popularity is that the Border tends to be more tolerant of children and other dogs than other Terriers, some of which can have a tendency to bark or snap.

Borders are intelligent and eager to please their owners. During training, they respond well to praise. They are ranked 30th in the Intelligence of Dogs, appearing in the 'Above Average Working Dogs' section. They learn quickly and respond well to obedience training, but must be kept engaged and well-exercised, as they are active dogs. If allowed to run free in the garden or yard, they need to be well fenced in, as their love of digging and jumping makes them expert escape artists.

This breed loves to be engaged; a dog left alone for long periods may well become destructive or resort to excessive barking. However, given the exercise and attention they need, Border Terriers make wonderful, loving companions who are happy and full of fun. Like all Terriers, they make excellent watchdogs and will bark if somebody comes to the door. But only take one on if you have the time and energy to deal with their lively personalities.

The hardy Border Terrier has an all-weather double coat. A short, dense undercoat is covered with a hard and wiry outer coat. This can be red, blue and tan, grizzle and tan or wheaten (pale yellow or fawn). Some have a small patch of white on the chest. They are regarded as low shedders and require only weekly brushing, but should be hand stripped a couple of times a year. Although not hypoallergenic, the low shedding wiry coat may make the breed suitable for some allergy sufferers; read the chapter on **Puppies for Allergy Sufferers** to find out how to tell if a specific Border Terrier pup might be suitable.

Listed in Breed Watch Category 1, the Border is a relatively healthy dog. Health issues include joint problems, heart murmur (which affects many small breed dogs), and eye problems. Ask to see hip and eye screening certificates.

SUMMARY: Hardy, lively Terrier with bags of energy and character who will chase small animals and may bark a lot. Needs daily exercise.

Boxer

The Boxer traces his roots back over hundreds of years through the Molossus, or Mastiff, a large working dog. In more recent times, the breed was developed in Germany in the late 19th century, where his direct ancestor was the Brabant Bullenbeisser (bull biter).

The Boxer is also a cousin of the Bulldog, a smaller type of Mastiff. They were bred to hunt and then hold on to the prey with their powerful jaws, and later also used as guard dogs. The name reputedly comes from the breed's tendency to play by standing on its hind legs and 'boxing' with its front paws.

Today's Boxer is a large dog which still retains his impressive, athletic appearance. Don't get a Boxer if you want a quiet life, Boxers approach life full-on. They are boisterous, lively, and full of fun.

Some owners would even say that a young Boxer can act a little crazy – he will certainly make you laugh with his antics. They can be extremely rewarding dogs, but must only be considered by owners who can give them the time and exercise they need to be content.

Exuberance, boundless energy and a desire to please sum up this versatile breed, especially when young. Many slow down as they age but, like the Bulldog, the Boxer does not reach maturity until about three years old. They tend to be very good with children, being patient and playful as well as protective, making them a popular choice for families.

These are active, strong dogs which require plenty of exercise to avoid their nemesis – boredom - which can result in destructive chewing, digging or licking. I know of one family who left their young Boxer alone for long periods while they went out to work and the dog ended up chewing its way through several kitchen cabinets.

Boxers are intelligent, but are listed only at 48th - in the 'Average Working/Obedience' Intelligence' section - of the Intelligence of Dogs list. This is because they can be headstrong and require a firm and patient hand when training. Some owners disagree with this rating and have found that with reward-based training methods,

Boxers have far above-average intelligence and working ability. It's important to make the time to train a young Boxer, so that his charming and playful boisterousness does not develop into uncontrolled energy as a big adult dog. Puppy classes are an excellent way of training and socialising at the same time, and this should be backed up with further socialisation sessions, especially when young.

The Kennel Club recommends more than two hours a day exercise for the breed, which loves a physical and mental challenge. A Boxer is a good choice if you are fit and spend a lot of time outdoors; they were bred as working dogs with plenty of muscle and stamina.

They are canine athletes and many excel in agility, obedience and other sports. Because of their strength and courage, they are used for military, police and search-and-rescue work, and some are specifically trained as guard dogs.

The Boxer makes a good watchdog and will bark when somebody comes to the house. How they act to strangers varies and will largely depend on how they have been socialised. The breed is not aggressive by nature and generally gets on well with smaller dogs and puppies, but may not respond so well to large dogs, particularly of the same sex. Like all dogs, the Boxer requires proper socialisation with other dogs and people.

These are companion dogs and do not do well when left alone for long periods; they are known for being extremely loyal and loving to their humans and often get on well with other dogs in the household. They have a sleek and short low-maintenance coat, which sheds but requires little grooming. The coat may be fawn or brindle, with or without white markings. In the USA, many have their ears cropped and tails docked. They are not a suitable breed for allergy sufferers.

Despite being a working dog, the Boxer is not suited to outdoor living. This is due to his short, fine coat and the fact that he is a brachycephalic (flat faced) breed, none of which tolerate extremes of temperature. If you are house-proud, a Boxer may not be the breed for you, they drool, snuffle, snore and are gassy!

They are listed in Breed Watch Category 1, no particular points of concern. But if you are buying a pup, check his or her breathing – does it sound relaxed or laboured? Health issues include cancers, aortic stenosis (a heart problem), hypothyroidism, hip dysplasia and epilepsy. Ask a breeder about hip dysplasia and hypothyroidism. They are also prone to environmental and food allergies. Average lifespan is 10 to 12 years.

SUMMARY: A big, boisterous, lovable dog which needs plenty of physical and mental stimulation and a firm hand when training. Buy from healthy stock, many have shortened lives due to health problems.

Miniature Schnauzer

The Miniature Schnauzer is the most popular of the three Schnauzer breeds. The Schnauzer originated in Southern Germany in the 14th or 15th century when farmers and traders travelled around selling their skills and produce at markets. They needed a medium-sized, versatile dog, strong enough to guard the cart, but small enough to easily fit into it. These practical men also wanted a good ratter to keep down the vermin back at home.

They probably crossed the black German Poodle and the grey Wolfspitz with more than a pinch of Wire-Haired Pinscher. This 'prototype' most closely resembled today's Standard Schnauzer, and the Miniature Schnauzer was bred down from this, probably with Affenpinschers, and first exhibited as a separate breed in 1899.

In the USA, they are classed as Terriers, while they are in the Utility Group in the UK. Having owned a Mini for 10 years, I think they definitely have Terrier-like tendencies, especially when it comes to chasing small animals and birds. They also love to get their heads down and wander off after a scent. Many will live happily with cats and other small animals, but usually need to be introduced at an early age.

These stylish dogs are generally perky, playful, extrovert and very affectionate. Some owners would even say they have a sense of humour. They are adaptable and at home both in town and country.

They need a medium amount of exercise – the exact amount will vary depending on what they have got used to - however, at least 30 to 45 minutes a day is recommended. When he was younger, ours was happy to go hiking all day.

However, if you are looking for a jogging partner, the Standard Schnauzer is a better choice.

This is a handsome breed with a square, boxy shape and unique beard. Physically, these dogs combine elegance with a certain ruggedness and a jaunty gait. They are minimal shedders with a double coat, the outer coat trapping the dander, and this is a breed which allergy sufferers can consider. However, allergies are very individual things and you have to spend time with the specific puppy you are considering. The coat needs hand stripping or trimming every eight weeks, which is another expense to consider, and ears require regular cleaning as the small hairy ear canals are prone to infection.

Accepted coat colours are pepper and salt, black, and black and silver. White Minis are becoming increasingly popular, but are not accepted by the Kennel Clubs. There is no such thing as a 'teacup' Schnauzer, this is a marketing term used by breeders of undersized Schnauzers, and health problems have been reported with some 'teacups'.

Minis make good watchdogs and, although they may be quiet as puppies, they get more vociferous as they grow in confidence. Adults will usually bark when somebody knocks at the door, and most will then greet the intruder like a long lost friend. They are not by nature laid-back dogs, so don't expect them to be happy to snooze in a corner all day. They want to be involved and demand your attention. If you have a garden, you'll have to fence them in to stop them running off in pursuit of small animals and birds, or simply to say hello to passers-by.

Mini Schnauzers want to be with humans, they love being part of the family and form strong bonds with their owners. They definitely don't like being left alone and can suffer from separation anxiety if not trained to be apart from their humans for short periods from an early age. They often do well with another Schnauzer or dog in the household.

Early training and socialisation is important. Get them used to other dogs and people, traffic, loud noises and other new experiences. Some Minis are frightened of loud bangs, but socialisation can help. They are often easily distracted by people, other dogs or interesting smells, so training should be kept short and fun. They are, however, intelligent and have a great desire to please their owners, so they generally soon pick up new commands and housetraining. They are listed as the 12th most intelligent dog in the Intelligence of Dogs list.

Minis thrive on their owners' attention and may even follow them around the house. They like to sleep on the bed or at least in the same room, when allowed. They make excellent companions, but given too much attention and a free rein, can develop 'Little Emperor' or 'Small Dog Syndrome' and become stubborn, attention-seeking and even snappy.

It's sometimes easy to forget that they are canines and not humans, and difficult not to form strong emotional bonds with these affectionate little dogs that become members of the family. But it's important to keep training going throughout their lifetime to remind them every now and again that you are in charge. Properly trained and socialised, they make delightful companions.

They are listed in Breed Watch Category 1 with no major points of concern. Diets should be low in fat and sugars to avoid potential problems and health issues to ask a breeder about are cataracts, diabetes, Cushing's disease, bladder stones and pancreatitis. Skin issues caused by environmental allergies are not uncommon in Minis, including ours. These can usually be managed with tablets and food supplements. Ask the breeder if the parents have any history of allergies. For more information visit www.max-the-schnauzer.com or read **The Schnauzer Handbook** http://amzn.to/1uNQGjx for detailed information on the breed.

SUMMARY: Stylish and playful breed with a perky personality. Some are more Terrier-like than others, check the temperament of the parents. Also ask breeders if there is a history of skin problems or allergies. A possibility for allergy sufferers.

Shih Tzu

The exact origins of this breed are unknown, but they stretch back some 3,000 years. The Shih Tzu is thought to have originated in Tibet and developed in China as a result of crossing the Lhasa Apso and Pekingese. The Shih Tzu was the house pet for most of the Ming Dynasty and they were so prized that the Chinese refused to sell or give away any of the dogs for many years.

The first were imported into Europe (England and Norway) in 1930, and classified as "Apsos" by the Kennel Club. The European breed standard was written in England in 1935 by the Shih Tzu Club. The breed was introduced to the United States after World War II, when returning soldiers brought the dogs back from Europe. The American Kennel Club recognised the Shih Tzu in 1969 and classed it in the Toy Group; it is in the Utility Group in the UK. The name comes from the Chinese for "lion dog."

As with most breeds, the temperament of the individual Shih Tzu varies from one to the next. However, the breed's typical character is loyal, affectionate, extravert and alert.

The Shih Tzu was bred solely as a companion dog for occupiers of the palaces and he is sweet natured and generally friendly and trusting with all people, including strangers.

In contrast, the similar-looking Lhasa Apso was bred to alert monks to intruders inside Buddhist temples, and can be wary of strangers until he gets to know them. Shih Tzu tend to be a bit more playful and affectionate than the Lhasa, which may be bolder. Both breeds are confident and cheerful.

The Shih Tzu loves to carry himself in a haughty manner with his head and tail held high, and looks resplendent when just groomed. Their nickname in 1930s England was 'the chrysanthemum dog', and the breed standard calls for a chrysanthemum face, meaning that the hair should grow in all difference directions. The coat of the Shih Tzu may come in many different colours, but all have long, fine hair.

Although there is no such thing as a non-shedding dog, the breed is a minimal shedder and is suitable for consideration by allergy sufferers (as is the Lhasa). He has a beautiful coat, but the downside is that it needs daily grooming to prevent matting, so you will have to allow time for this. You'll also have to factor in the expense of a trip to the groomer's every few weeks.

Some owners favour the sheared look as it is easier to keep clean and tangle-free. The Shih Tzu's facial wrinkles and ears also need to be cleaned regularly by the owner.

On the positive side, this is a breed which, despite being sturdy, requires little exercise as it is not particularly active, being more of a lap dog. He's happy as long as he's with you and a couple of short walks a day are enough, The Kennel Club describes the exercise requirement as "up to an hour a day," making Shih Tzu suitable for the elderly or for people who live in apartments.

The Shih Tzu is listed 70th, two places below the Lhasa, in The Intelligence of Dogs list. The breed is in the 'Lowest Degree of Working/Obedience Intelligence' category. Some are not the easiest of dogs to train, they can have a stubborn streak. It is worth putting the time in early on to teach the Shih Tzu basic commands and manners around the house.

They are notoriously difficult to housetrain, so vigilance is needed early on to ensure that this does not become an issue. Some dogs eat faeces (coprophagia) and for some inexplicable reason, Shi Tzu can be particularly prone to doing this. Clean up poo(p) regularly and keep cat litter trays out of reach.

The Shih Tzu is in Breed Watch Category 1, no major points of concern. But like all brachycephalic (flat faced) breeds - including the Lhasa Apso - Shih Tzu can easily overheat, some may have difficulty breathing and anaesthetic can present a risk. Choose a puppy that appears to breathe normally and a veterinarian who is familiar with brachycephalic breeds.

For walks, use a harness rather than a collar, as this can exert pressure on the narrow windpipe. Other health issues include allergies, hip dysplasia and eye problems (ask to see the breeder's health screening certificates for these two issues), congenital liver shunt, teeth and gum problems, and disk disease.

If you are looking for a puppy, be aware that there is no such breed as an 'imperial' or 'teacup' Shih Tzu. These are terms used by unrecognised breeders to describe oversized or undersized pups they have bred and should be avoided. Choose an accredited breeder. The Shih Tzu is long lived, from 10 to 16 years. A UK Kennel Club survey puts the average life span at 13 years and 2 months.

SUMMARY: Characterful companion dog who likes to be with people and has low exercise requirements. The breed can be difficult to housetrain. He's a sweet companion dog in households where the owner - not the dog - is pack leader. A possibility for allergy sufferers.

Lhasa Apso

The Lhasa Apso has a fascinating history. It was bred as an indoor watch dog to alert monks in Buddhist monasteries to any intruders who entered. The breed's keen hearing and sharp bark warned the monks, like a modern day burglar alarm, if an intruder got past the exterior guards, which were often Mastiffs. Lhasa Apso means 'long-haired dog from Lhasa', the capital of Tibet.

Incredibly, the Lhasa Apso originated over 4,000 years ago as a small breed of mountain wolf. They were domesticated and actively bred as long ago as 800 BC, which makes it one of the 14 oldest dog breeds in the world. Despite most people thinking of the Lhasa as a cuddly lap dog, recent research has shown it to be one of the breeds most closely related to the ancestral wolf.

Some of the breed's physical characteristics - such as the head and body structure, dense double coat which flows over the eyes, and muscled body - have evolved as a result of the breed's native land and climate. High altitudes, a dry windy climate, dusty terrain, short hot summer and long bitterly cold winter of the Himalayas have all led to the dog we see today.

Tibetans believed that the bodies of Lhasas could be entered by souls of deceased lamas (holy men, not woolly camelids) while they awaited rebirth into a new body and so they were never sold, only ever given as a gift. In the early 1900s, a few were brought to England by soldiers returning from the Indian subcontinent, they then were called the Lhasa Terrier. Today the Lhasa is classed in the Utility Group in the UK and the Non-Sporting Group in the USA (unlike the Shih Tzu, which is classed in the Toy Group in the USA).

Referred to in Tibet as the Bearded Lion Dog, this is also how the dog sees himself. It is said that when a Lhasa Apso looks in the mirror, he sees a lion, as the adult Lhasa is one of the hardiest, toughest and strongest-willed of all the small breeds. He was bred to do a job, to guard the monastery, rather than as a companion (as the Shih Tzu was) and still retains some of these inherited characteristics.

Some have a heightened sense of hearing and other senses, and many like jumping up on to the furniture to get a good look-out position – especially if they are awaiting your return. This breed is not suitable for people out of the home a lot. Lhasas thrive on being with their owners and families; many develop separation anxiety if left alone too long. If you get one, start by leaving your puppy for short periods and then gradually add a few minutes to the length of time you are absent.

Like the Shih Tzu, the Lhasa carries himself in an imperial manner, but unlike the Shih Tzu, Lhasas can be wary of strangers and even aggressive towards them if not properly trained. They require socialisation with other dogs and people, not only as puppies, but throughout their lives.

Listed 68th, two places above the Shih Tzu, in The Intelligence of Dogs list, the breed is in the 'Lowest Degree of Working/Obedience Intelligence' category. Despite having an independent streak, Lhasas do like to please their owners and generally enjoy training sessions –

provided they are not too long. They require patience when housebreaking, as they can sometimes taken months to get the hang of it. Early vigilance is the key.

So what's the attraction - apart from their incredibly appealing looks? Well, there are many. They are fiercely loyal to their owners and, as long as they know who is boss and are properly socialised, they make wonderful, entertaining companions with relatively few health problems. They are spirited and affectionate and with training, very obedient with their owners.

However, like all small dogs, they can develop "Little Emperor Syndrome" if allowed to rule the household, and this manifests itself in barking and even snapping. Treat this hardy little chap like a dog, not a child and you will be rewarded with a loyal and affectionate companion.

The breed has a dense, double coat, which flows straight and long over the entire body, including the head and eyes, to the floor. This is a breed for consideration by allergy sufferers. Any colour of coat is acceptable in the show ring, where this handsome dog excels, but gold, cream and honey are the most popular. The coat may also be dark-grizzle, slate, smoke and multi-colours of brown, white and black.

Puppy coats often change colour as the dog grows. Daily grooming is required to prevent knots and tangles, which is why many owners who do not show their Lhasas have their hair cut short. The cost of a trip to the groomers should be factored in when buying a Lhasa.

This breed does not need much exercise, although will happily walk for miles over any terrain. He has a jaunty gait and carries his head high in a regal fashion, all set off by his beautiful plumed tail.

The Lhasa Apso is in Breed Watch Category 1, no major points of concern. But like all brachycephalic (flat faced) breeds, some can experience breathing problems and all overheat easily. Anaesthesia can also pose a risk, so choose a free-breathing puppy and then a vet familiar with brachycephalic breeds. A Lhasa has a thick coat and should be monitored in hot weather. Generally, this breed is regarded as one of the healthiest, although some suffer from sebaceous adenitis, a hereditary skin disease. Eye conditions can be another issue, ask to see the breeder's eye screening certificates.

Lhasas are long lived, some have even reached 20 years old. A Kennel Club survey put the median lifespan at 14 years 4 months, while data from a UK vet clinic put it at 13 years exactly.

SUMMARY: A hardy, loyal companion with a strong character. Suitable for apartment life and for consideration by allergy sufferers. Some can be difficult to housetrain.

Cavalier King Charles Spaniel

The Cavalier King Charles is the only Spaniel not classed in the Gundog Group. Instead it is listed in the Toy Group by the major Kennel Clubs. It is one of the most popular breeds in the UK and is now in the top 20 in the US.

The Cavvie's ancestors are the small Spaniels seen in so many famous paintings dating back to the 16th, 17th and 18th centuries. In the 1500s Toy Spaniels were quite common as ladies' pets, and King Charles II (1630-1685) was so fond of his little Spaniels that he decreed they should be accepted in any public place - even the Houses of Parliament - and this still stands today.

It was during the late 1700s that the King Charles Cavalier Spaniel changed radically when it was interbred with flat-nosed (brachycephalic) breeds. It is said that all modern Cavaliers can trace their ancestry back to six dogs and, sadly, the breed is affected by a number of inherited defects. Cavaliers were one of the breeds featured on the 2008 BBC programme **Pedigree Dogs Exposed**.

This highlighted the breed's suffering caused by a distressing neurological condition called syringomyelia, resulting from having a large brain in a small skull and thought to affect up to half of all CKCs. The other major issue affecting almost all Cavvies is an inherited heart condition called mitral valve disease - the number one killer of the breed. Do not consider buying a Cavvie puppy unless you see the breeder's health screening certificates for these problems. The breed is in Breed Watch Category 1.

The Cavvie is smaller than other Spaniels and in character is a cross between a lap dog and a sporting dog. He is first and foremost a companion and is entirely dependent on humans for his happiness, so don't consider one if you are out at work all day; he won't be happy. On the other hand, he needs more exercise than other dogs in the Toy group. The Kennel Club recommends up to an hour a day.

Cavvies are fairly adaptable, some love to take part in organised activities, while others are more sedate, they tend to take after their owners in this respect. As long as they are regularly exercised every day, they can be suitable for apartment life. They do, however, have a natural instinct to chase small animals and birds. And early socialisation is important to prevent them from becoming too timid.

The CKC is an affectionate, undemanding and easy to train family dog which does well with children. Care should be taken with young children and puppies, as the pups are very small and delicate. Temperaments vary within the breed, some will bark at visitors, many won't. They are generally friendly with everyone, their tails wag constantly and they are very affectionate, loving to snuggle up in your lap – if you'll let them. They are lower down the Intelligence of Dogs list than most other Spaniels, number 44 in the 'Average Working/Obedience Intelligence' section. They are, however, generally easy to train and quick to housetrain.

Their coat is long and silky with plenty of feathering, and comes in colours with marvellous names: Blenheim (rich chestnut), Black and Tan, Ruby and Tricolour. It requires regular grooming and ear cleaning to prevent infections. The breed is regarded as high shedding and is not at all suitable for allergy sufferers. Regular trips to the grooming salon for a trim and clean-up will have to be factored in when considering this gentle, handsome breed. Lifespan for a healthy Cavvie is over 12 years.

SUMMARY: The Cavvie is a sweet, well-mannered dog with lower exercise requirements than other Spaniels, although they still need a couple of walks a day. Choose your puppy carefully, with health being the main consideration.

Dachshund

Strictly speaking, this is not one breed, but six! There are two sizes (Standard and Miniature) and three coat types (Long-Haired, Smooth-Haired and Wire-Haired). The name means 'badger dog' in German and all are classed in the Hound Group by the Kennel Clubs. Some breed experts argue that with their love of digging and feisty personality, Dachshunds - particularly the Wire-Haired - have characteristics more akin to the Terrier Group.

In the UK, the Miniature Smooth-Haired Dachshund is the most popular of all the six types. The Wire-Haired is the least popular coat in the US, despite being the most common in Germany and the most recent to appear in breed standards.

Some historians believe the early roots of the Dachshund can be traced as far back as Ancient Egypt, following discovery of engravings featuring short-legged hunting dogs. The earliest specific references appear in 18th century books when they were originally called a 'Dachs Kriecher' (badger crawler) or 'Dachs Krieger' (badger warrior). The original German dogs were bigger, weighing 30lb to 40lb, and were either straight-legged or crook-legged - modern Dachshunds are descended from the crooked-legged type.

With his long body, short legs and paddle-like paws for digging, the standard Dachshund was bred to scent, chase and flush out badgers and other burrow-dwelling animals.

His distinctive shape has also led to the nickname of Wiener or Sausage Dog - my neighbour has even called her Dachshund 'Sizzles,' after the sound of sausages frying! The Miniature Dachshund was developed to hunt smaller prey, such as rabbits, and in the American West they have also been used in hunting prairie dogs. Today they are bred as family pets and for showing, although some participate in earthdog trials in North America.

Like all hounds, the Dachshund has a keen sense of smell and he'll be off after a small animal or bird as quick as he can. Make sure he is on the lead near traffic as, like a Terrier, he'll dash off after anything moving, regardless of whether cars are in the way or not. Dachshunds are lively and playful; little dogs with a lot of character. The Americans call them "spunky", the Brits have a rather more reserved description: "courageous and determined." They love games and chase balls with great determination.

A Dachshund is bold and pretty sure of himself, resulting in many being stubborn and a challenge to train. American writer E. B. White wrote: "I would rather train a striped zebra to balance an Indian club than induce a dachshund to heed my slightest command. When I address Fred I never have to raise either my voice or my hopes. He even disobeys me when I instruct him in something he wants to do."

Boldness and independent minds are part of these dogs' character and appeal. The AKC states: "The Dachshund is clever, lively, and courageous to the point of rashness, persevering in above and below ground work, with all the senses well-developed. Any display of shyness is a serious fault."

Dachshunds are at number 49 in the Intelligence of Dogs list, in the 'Average Working/Obedience Intelligence' section. Although they don't need a great deal of exercise (up to 30 minutes a day), they can easily become bored, so a good owner ensures their 'Doxie' has plenty of entertainment and enough walks to keep him stimulated. Despite their size, Dachshunds have a relatively loud, deep bark, which they use frequently, making them excellent watchdogs - but sometimes a tad annoying for the neighbours.

They are loyal companions which can become very attached to one person. Early socialisation helps to prevent them becoming jealous and snappy with other people or dogs. For them to get on with a young child, a cat or other animal, it is a good idea to introduce them while the Dachshund is still a puppy. Unsocialised dogs may be tempted to nip a toddler. They often do well with other dogs, especially other Dachshunds and many owners have more than one. Left alone for long periods, Dachshunds can also suffer from separation anxiety and may whine or chew.

Although the Wire-Haired sheds less than the other varieties, none of the six breeds are hypoallergenic and therefore are not suitable for allergy sufferers. Grooming requirements are fairly minimal for the Smooth-Haired, while the Long-Haired needs more regular brushing. The Wire-Haired is a low shedder, but needs hand stripping or clipping every few weeks.

All Standard Dachshunds are in Breed Watch Category 1, while Miniatures are in Category 2 with the point of concern listed as "body weight/condition." If you are looking to get a puppy, the stand-out feature should be the short legs, not an extra-long back, which can cause health problems. One in four Dachshunds suffer from spinal problems, particularly intervertebral disk disease (IVDD). The problem will be made worse by obesity (not uncommon with Dachshunds), jumping on to furniture, rough handling and intense exercise. Lifespan is 12 to 15 years.

SUMMARY: In very general terms, the Wire-Haired tend to be the most energetic, mischievous and obstinate, probably due to the fact that they are thought to have some Terrier ancestry. Long-Haired Dachshunds tend to be the quietest and sweetest-natured – this may be attributable to their Spaniel ancestors – and the Smooth-Haired is most likely to be a one-person dog and less friendly with strangers. Miniature Dachshunds are often more active than Standards and other breeds are more suitable with very small children.

Poodle

The Poodle is not a single breed either, but three breeds: the Standard, Miniature and Toy Poodle. No round-up of dog breeds would be complete without discussing the Poodle, which has become extremely popular not only as a pedigree (purebred) dog in its own right, but has also been mated with other breeds to create many highly popular crossbreeds in recent years (much to the displeasure of pedigree Poodle breeders). The Poodle has been the stud of choice due to his unique coat with its non-shedding (technically, low-shedding) properties.

The Poodle is a water dog which originated in Germany, where its name – Pudelhund – meant 'splash in water dog'. The Standard Poodle is considered the original and was a gundog used mainly for hunting duck and sometimes upland birds. Large Poodles have featured in paintings dating back to the 15th century.

Although developed in Germany, the breed was standardised in France, where its popularity led to it becoming the national breed. There is some evidence that the smaller types developed only a short time after the large Poodle.

The Toy Poodle, the smallest of the three, was known in England as early as the 18th century. All three types are classed in the Utility Group in the UK. In the US, the Standard and Miniature (which is actually medium-sized) are in the Non-Sporting Group, while the Toy is unsurprisingly classed in the Toy Group.

Apart from his striking appearance, the Poodle has two other outstanding features: his coat and his intelligence. Yes, the Poodle has beauty AND brains! After the Border Collie, the Poodle is the most intelligent canine on the planet, according to the Intelligence of Dogs List.

One of the biggest misconceptions is that Poodles, with their often elaborate hairstyles, are somehow 'soppy' dogs. Nothing could be further from the truth – these clever, handsome dogs are full of character, as any owner will testify.

Poodles have been used as working dogs in the military since at least the 17th century, and in 1942 the Poodle was one of 32 breeds officially classified as war dogs by the Army. Due to their intelligence, they need plenty of challenges in the form of both physical and mental stimulation. You don't want a bored Poodle on your hands. Many Standards in particular are boisterous, lively dogs which need a lot of exercise and challenge. They excel at agility and obedience classes, being both athletic and highly intelligent.

All Poodles – even small ones - like to run, play and swim, and exercise is a necessity for their happiness. With a Standard this may be one to two hours a day. Miniature and Toy Poodles require less, it will vary from one individual dog to the next. All Poodles are among the easiest to train of all the breeds.

They pick up obedience, housetraining and tricks easily – and indeed, most love being the centre of attention and showing off their skills. Make sure to spend the time housetraining, some males have a tendency to mark their territory - and that can be indoors if not educated otherwise.

All three types are attentive to their owners and some are 'intuitive', picking up on their owner's moods. Because of this, some Poodles do not respond well to stress, tension, and loud noises. When choosing a puppy, go for one whose parents have calm temperaments, as some bloodlines can produce highly strung offspring.

They are also not dogs you can leave all day as they thrive on interaction with their owners and may suffer from separation anxiety if left alone too long. The Standard will get on with children if introduced properly and the youngsters are not allowed to taunt him. Miniatures and Toys may have less patience with young children, with their accompanying antics and high noise levels. All Poodles should be properly socialised with other dogs and people, the smaller ones can become snappy and selfish if allowed to rule the roost, so puppy classes are recommended.

The Poodle's coat is the reason he has become so popular as one half of crosses such as the Labradoodle, Goldendoodle and Cockapoo. All three types of Poodle have a single layer coat of dense, curly fur almost like fleece. They shed hardly at all, are regarded as hypoallergenic and are suitable for consideration by allergy sufferers. The coat is beautiful when cared for and can be trimmed into a variety of exotic styles, or simply trimmed short for easy care.

The Poodle's is a coat of many colours. Solids include white, cream, black, brown, silver, grey, silver beige, apricot and red. Non-solid colours, such as parti (white and another colour), are NOT accepted by the Kennel Clubs, so if you buy one of these colours, the dog will not be Kennel Club registered or produced by an accredited breeder.

All Poodles are extremely high maintenance when it comes to grooming, requiring daily care to prevent the coat from becoming tangled and matted. The insides of ears should be cleaned and plucked regularly, as ear infections are common. They also need a visit to the groomer's every few weeks for a trim, which will add up to several hundred pounds - or dollars - a year.

Poodles are regarded as relatively healthy breeds. They are in Breed Watch Category 1, with no major points of concern. Health issues include Addison's disease (a hormonal problem), bloat, thyroid and skin problems, epilepsy and hip dysplasia.

SUMMARY: This highly intelligent and sensitive dog is highly rewarding if you can give him the time and stimulation he needs. Many Poodles prefer a quiet household which is not too stressful for them, so a different breed would be a better choice if you have a busy household full of noisy children. The breed is hypoallergenic.

Chihuahua

The Chihuahua's claim to fame is that he is the smallest of all the dog breeds - but he compensates by having a big personality. He is also the oldest recognised breed in the Americas. Unsurprisingly, these diminutive dogs are classed in the Toy Group by all the Kennel Clubs.

There are two types: the Long-Coated Chihuahua - the most popular type in the UK - and the Smooth-Coated Chihuahua (called Long-Haired and Short-Haired in the USA). They are classed as two breeds in the UK, despite being very similar apart from coat, and two types of the same breed in the USA.

The history of the Chihuahua has fuelled much debate. It is thought that the breed was already present at the time of the Toltec civilisation in ninth century Mexico and that it is a descendent of the Techichi, a slightly larger and sturdier dog. What is known is that the Chihuahua takes its name from the Mexican state of the same name.

In the US, the breed first became popular in bordering states such as Texas, New Mexico and Arizona before spreading across the rest of the continent. The Chihuahua is one of the oldest registered breeds in the US. A Chihuahua called Midget was the first to be officially registered by the American Kennel Club in 1904, just 20 years after the formation of the AKC.

When picking a puppy it is extremely important to make your decision based on a number of factors: the breeder's track record, health certificates and the temperament of the parents. This is especially true of Chihuahuas, where their temperament varies enormously, with the biggest single factor being the temperament of the parents. Often these dogs are lively and bold, but some may be timid, while others are more sedate.

Chihuahuas are complex characters. They are generally entertaining, extremely loyal to their owners and eager to give and receive affection from them. They make great companion dogs as they form such a strong bond with their owners and require little exercise – up to 30 minutes a day is enough - making them suitable for the elderly. They get exercise running round the house and garden, but all dogs have a need to 'migrate' and this is satisfied with a daily walk away from the home enjoying new experiences and places to sniff.

They are also very fond of snuggling up and sleeping under the covers with you, if you allow them to. All Chihuahuas shed, although not very much, but nevertheless they are not regarded as suitable for allergy sufferers. A Chihuahua can appear to be a calm even-tempered dog until somebody new knocks on your door, and if you have more than one they will bark in unison. One of the downsides of some Chihuahuas is that they are very noisy, barking at the slightest thing. Early socialisation is the key.

The main factor, other than parentage, governing your Chihuahua's character is how you socialise and train him. A well-socialised and trained Chi is a delight to live with. From puppyhood get them used to different people, dogs, noises and experiences to help them become less suspicious.

Teach them to respect their place in the household, and, above all, treat them like a dog, not a baby. They are strong willed and can be difficult to train, listed at number 67 in the Intelligence of Dogs, just scraping into the 'Fair Working/Obedience Intelligence' section.

The best way to train a Chihuahua is to get him engaged by persuading him that what you are doing is fun. Praise and food are powerful training tools, this breed does not respond well to shouting.

 Training is essential if you don't want your little Chi to develop 'Small Dog Syndrome,' where he becomes manipulative and rules the roost, resulting in him being a pain in the you-know-what to live with. Aggression from a dog is not comical and should not be tolerated, no matter how small the dog.

Interestingly, Chihuahuas seem to prefer other Chihuahuas to other dog breeds, towards whom they can be aggressive if not socialised as a pup. They can have very delicate legs and some may be unpredictable around youngsters, so this breed is not recommended if you have small children. They also don't tolerate cold very well, or being left along for long periods, as they have been bred as companion dogs. In short, don't baby your Chi. Properly treated and knowing his place in the household, he will be an affectionate companion.

There are no such things as teacup, miniature or micro Chihuahuas. These are names invented by breeders who create under-sized examples of the breed. Chihuahuas are small enough already. Inexperienced breeders meddling about with genetics by making size the only consideration only leads to health and temperament problems. Buy a Chihuahua within the breed standard guidelines (4lb to 6lb in the UK, 2lb to 6lb in the USA) from a breeder recommended by the Kennel Club in your country.

Another thing to look out for is the shape of the dog's head, only the apple shape is accepted by the Kennel Clubs. If you want to show your dog, it should have a well-rounded domed head like an apple. The deer head is more elongated with a longer, narrower snout (more like a deer) and does not conform to the breed standard, resulting in disqualification from any show run under Kennel Club rules. A deer head Chihuahua typically has a longer body and legs than the apple head, but not always.

Chihuahuas are in Breed Watch Category 1, no major point of concern. Health issues include neurological issues such as seizures, hydrocephalus and low blood sugar. Choose a vet proficient with tiny Toy breeds.

SUMMARY: Teach him his place in the household and you will have a loving and loyal companion which requires little exercise. Above all, treat a Chihuahua like a dog, not a baby. Because of their size and delicate nature, they are not recommended for homes with small children.

Staffordshire Bull Terrier

Like the Bulldog and the Boxer, the origins of the Staffordshire Bull Terrier lie with the big Mastiffs way back in the mists of time. The breed today is a mixture of Bulldog and Terrier, created in the English Midlands in the 19th century.

The Bulldog was used for bull baiting and during these bloodthirsty bouts, these athletic, fearless dogs would hold on to the bull with their powerful jaws, often being tossed off and injured. In 1832 the sport was finally banned, and after that working men began crossing the courageous Bulldog with smaller, tenacious Terriers to create a dog to fight in dog pits – a less expensive and often clandestine sport which also took place in the US.

This dog was originally known as the Bull and Terrier. It had the powerful jaws and bravery of the Bulldog, but its Terrier heritage made the dog smaller, faster and more agile. A group of enthusiasts sought to adapt the Bull and Terrier to create an animal more suited to the show ring and family home. It became known as the Staffordshire Bull Terrier and was officially recognised in the UK in 1935, and in America in 1975. Today the 'Staffie' is classed in the Terrier Group.

The Staffordshire Bull Terrier is, perhaps, one of the most maligned breeds. There has been a tendency in recent years for some young men to keep these former fighting dogs – and dogs crossed with Staffies - as macho status symbols, encouraging them to be aggressive. This has led to some bad publicity for this much-loved breed. Like all powerful breeds, the Staffie needs proper handling. Yet with the right training and socialisation, he makes an excellent family companion.

RSPCA chief vet Mark Evans has said: "Staffies have had a terrible press, but this is not of their own making—in fact they're wonderful dogs. If people think that Staffies have problems, they're looking at the wrong end of the dog lead! When well cared for and properly trained they can make brilliant companions. Our experience suggests that problems occur when bad owners exploit the Staffie's desire to please by training them to show aggression."

The original Staffordshire Bull Terriers were trained to be highly aggressive with other dogs, but placid enough with people to allow them to be handled. A much toned-down version sums up the natural instincts of the breed today: wonderful with adults and children, but can show aggression towards other dogs if not properly socialised. Some will chase cats and never get along with other animals in the house, while others socialise well if introduced at an early age. If you have other pets, you need to make sure the Staffie will get on with them before committing yourself to the puppy.

The Staffie is a muscular, athletic dog, with males often being somewhat bigger than females. Energy levels vary from one dog to the next depending on what they get used to, but an hour a day is recommended for most. The breed has stamina and if you're a fitness or outdoors enthusiast, a Staffie will happily get used to more. Exercise is important to keep his muscles toned and to prevent obesity, which the breed is prone to.

They are not recommended for apartment living due to their exercise requirements and if you have a garden or yard, make sure you have a high fence around it – this dog can jump and dig as well as run, which is why most love agility and obedience competitions. The breed has plenty of character and enthusiasm for life, loves to be stroked and is surprisingly sensitive for such a tough looking canine. Expect to be nuzzled, licked and nudged by your Staffie.

At home he is gentle, affectionate and adaptable. Like the Bulldog, the Staffie loves his family, especially children, and has even been nicknamed the 'Nanny Dog' because of his devotion to them. Inside the home he loves nothing better than assuming the role of couch potato on your couch - where else? – surrounded by his family. As with all dogs, time spent with young children should be supervised.

He has been bred to be a companion dog and thrives on being with people, he dislikes being left alone for extended periods. Left to his own devices he may well chew and his powerful jaws can inflict some serious damage on your prize possessions. All Staffies chew, especially when young, so buy a selection of durable toys he can work his way through.

The Staffie is not mentioned in The intelligence of Dogs although his cousin, the American Staffordshire Terrier, just makes it into the top half of the list in the 'Above Average Working Dogs' section. Like all Bully breeds, the Staffie can be an independent thinker and have a stubborn streak, so he needs to learn his position in the household – and that should be below you.

Obedience training and socialisation with other dogs and people should be an absolute priority. Don't let him off the lead until he has learned to behave around other dogs. Training should be reward-based - never punishment-based - and a firm but patient approach is the best method.

The Staffordshire Bull Terrier has a low-maintenance short, smooth coat which requires a weekly brush and sheds a little, so is not suitable for allergy sufferers. Colours can be red, fawn, white, black or blue or any one of these with white, as well as brindle or brindle with white. Staffies should not be kept outdoors, they are a brachycephalic breed and do not tolerate heat or cold.

Classed in Breed Watch Category 2, the points of concern are: "Difficulty breathing, Misplaced lower canine teeth." Ask the breeder about screening certificates for hereditary cataracts and L2HGA, a metabolic disorder. A UK Kennel Club survey puts the median lifespan at 12.75 years, while UK vet clinic data puts it at 10.

SUMMARY: This breed does not deserve its bad Press. With a responsible owner, socialisation with other dogs and training, this is a very loving and affectionate family dog which is good with children. Generally healthy and low maintenance.

Whippet

The Whippet was bred to hunt by sight, coursing game over open land at high speed and the breed is descended from the Greyhound. References to this sleek hound go all the way back thousands of years to Ancient Egypt when the pharaohs bred a small sight hound to keep in their palaces. In medieval England a small type of greyhound became popular for ratting, but the first use of the word 'Whippet' to describe a type of dog was not until 1610.

The history of the breed involves an element of cruelty. The original Whippets were English Greyhounds that were too small for stag hunting in the forests. These dogs were often returned to their peasant breeders, who were not allowed to hunt, so the dogs were maimed - usually by cutting a leg tendon or removing the toes of one paw. However, the owners kept and bred these dogs, producing a smaller version of a Greyhound that was ideal for hunting rats, hares and rabbits. When the hunting laws changed, these small Greyhounds became very popular for coursing and dog racing and were known as 'snap dogs' for their tendency to snap up prey.

In the 1800s Whippet racing was a major sport, especially among coal miners and other working men in northern England and Wales, resulting in the nickname of 'the poor man's racehorse.' Whippet racing is still practised in the UK and USA - although these days the hare is electric - and the breed loves events such as agility, flyball and lure coursing. Despite being developed in Britain, the Whippet was recognised by the American Kennel Club first in 1888, followed by the (UK) Kennel Club three years later. The breed has since won Best in Show at both Crufts and Westminster.

The Whippet is a sight hound, it sees prey and runs... and runs... and runs! Pound for pound this dog is the fastest canine on the planet, reaching speeds of up to 35mph and weighing as little as 15lb – although American Whippets tend to be larger than their British cousins. If you are considering getting a Whippet, know that this dog is hard wired for speed and should be allowed to run free every day in order to be truly content. A Whippet in full flight is a joy to behold, when the true instinct of the dog is there for all to see. This natural athlete has it all: speed, poise, balance, style, elegance and a tremendous turn of speed over short distances.

Provided they get enough daily exercise, they are normally calm at home, being perfectly happy to snooze most of the rest of the day away. The Whippet is a charming dog, he can be summed up in three words: neat, sweet and fleet. Because early Whippets were bred to run with other dogs without fighting, they have an even temperament and usually do well with other canines. Being pack hounds they thrive in households with other dogs. They still have an extremely strong instinct to chase small animals, including cats, so if you already have a cat, a Whippet might not be a suitable choice.

These favourites of the working classes also endured cramped conditions with their humans and learned to live alongside them in a gentle and unobtrusive manner. They still like to be close to their humans and may follow their owner around the house or snuggle up on the couch. Being athletic and without much padding on their bones, they love a soft surface and can easily jump up on to furniture - or even kitchen worktops if there's food about - so train them not to jump up when they are young.

Generally the Whippet has more energy than a Greyhound and wants to be closer to his owners. He is amusing and playful in a gentle way, particularly when young. He should be trained and socialised, not only to get him used to other animals, but some Whippets can be highly strung (or over-sensitive) if not exposed to loud noises, traffic, new people and places early in their lives. He does not usually like rowdy households and can become frightened or stressed by too much noise. Indoors he is calm - although he might have an occasional mad five minutes, especially as a pup or adolescent. He is eager to please and with kindness and patience, should be relatively easy to train and housebreak.

Like other hounds, the Whippet has an independent mind, a minority can even be aloof. The Whippet is at number 51 with the Wire Fox Terrier in the 'Average Working/Obedience Intelligence' section of the Intelligence of Dogs list. The AKC says: "Amiable, friendly, gentle, but capable of great intensity during sporting pursuits." However well you train a Whippet, you may not be able to stop him racing after prey, such as squirrels or rabbits. Unless you are looking for a watch dog, the Whippet has another advantage over some breeds: many almost never bark. Some bark when they are excited, others may be vocal when demanding something from you. Whippets love company and one left alone too much may also bark and whine

The breed has a short coat and, unusually, any colour is acceptable. The fine coat requires only minimal grooming, as Whippets are generally very clean animals, but they should not be left outside as they feel the cold easily. They are light shedders and so generally not suitable for allergy sufferers.

The Whippet is a healthy breed, listed in Category 1 of Breed Watch. However, he may occasionally nick and tear his thin skin while racing around. The Whippet has a large heart, some have an arrhythmia and many breeders also screen for eye and hearing disorders. Like other sight hounds, they are intolerant of barbiturate anaesthetics.

SUMMARY: A quiet, gentle addition to the household. Some can be sensitive to loud noises, etc, and others may be aloof. They need to run free to be truly happy.

Yorkshire Terrier

The Yorkshire Terrier comes from Yorkshire in northern England. The breed was developed by weavers in the 1850s to catch rats in the textile mills and his ancestors were various Terrier breeds, including some from Scotland, as well as a dog similar to the Skye Terrier and possibly even the Maltese.

A dog named Huddersfield Ben born in 1865 became the top show and stud dog and is considered to be the father of the modern Yorkshire Terrier.

The breed was first recognised in the UK in 1870 and 15 years later in America. Today this handsome and perky canine is one of the most popular breeds in North America, being consistently in the top 10.

Despite being classed in the Toy group, this feisty little canine is a true Terrier. Weighing just four to seven pounds, the Yorkie is one of the smallest breeds, but makes up for his lack of size with an assertive personality. The AKC describes the desired temperament as: "Brave, determined, investigative and energetic," and adds: "The dog's high head carriage and confident manner should give the appearance of vigor and self-importance."

The Yorkie is full of himself, his natural tendency is to chase anything small - and often to confront dogs much bigger than himself. Socialisation with other animals and dogs in puppyhood is extremely important. If not, Yorkies can bark or show aggression towards other dogs, causing them to pick fights which they have no chance of winning and can end badly. They can also be hostile towards strangers if not socialised with other people.

They are undoubtedly attention seekers and very affectionate with their owners. Whether a Yorkie turns out to be a delightful little companion or a snappy little aggressor depends very much on his owner. Treat him like a dog, not like a baby. An over-pampered Yorkshire Terrier is a pain in the ass; yappy, possessive, protective of his owner and grumpy with everybody else.

On the other hand, a properly trained Yorkie is a joy, he is loving, spirited, fun and well-rounded. Temperaments vary from one bloodline to the next, with some being more highly strung than others. Discuss this with a breeder and choose a puppy from more laid-back parents.

Yorkies are the most intelligent of all Terriers according to Stanley Coren's Intelligence of Dogs. They are at number 27, just one position below the 'Excellent Working Dogs' section. Although easy to train with treats and encouragement, the Yorkshire can be difficult to housetrain. The secret to keeping him happy and well rounded - apart from training and socialisation - is to be around a lot of the time, a lonely Yorkshire becomes very grumpy, and give him enough daily exercise.

Despite being very small, he is still a canine and all have a natural need to migrate, or spend time outside the home. Up to 30 minutes a day is enough, making him eminently suitable for apartment living or as a companion for the elderly. The breed is tiny and delicate, and for this reason is not recommended for households with small children.

The Yorkie's stand out feature is his beautiful trademark coat. His silky hair must be glossy, fine and straight and is high maintenance. Traditionally the coat is grown very long and parted down the middle of the back, with some owners showing off their little companion with a topknot or ribbon.

To maintain the coat in optimum show condition requires regular expert grooming, so some owners have the coat regularly trimmed for easier care. Even if you are not showing your dog, daily grooming is required to keep the coat in tiptop condition and prevent matting. The good news is that the breed is regarded as hypoallergenic and therefore a suitable consideration for allergy sufferers, although anyone with allergies should spend time with the specific puppy before committing.

Puppies are born black and tan, showing an intermingling of black hair in the tan until they are matured, when the only acceptable colour is blue and tan. The blue is a dark steel blue, not silver blue and not mingled with fawn, bronze or black hairs. Prospective owners should be aware that these are the ONLY acceptable colours.

Some unaccredited breeders are charging high prices for "rare colours" - be aware **there is no such thing** and these dogs do not conform to breed standards. Similarly, there is no such thing as "teacup" Yorkshire Terriers. Undersized Yorkies weighing three pounds or less generally have a shorter life span, as they are especially prone to a range of health problems, including chronic diarrhoea and vomiting, they are even more sensitive to anaesthetic and more easily injured.

The Yorkie, although very sensitive to heat and cold, is fairly healthy, listed in Breed Watch Category 1 with no major points of concern. Generally the breed has delicate limbs and digestive system and does not always tolerate anaesthesia well, so choose a vet familiar with Toy breeds.

Unusually, the breed does not always lose its milk teeth when it should, so have your vet check the dog's mouth when visiting for regular check-ups or vaccinations. Other health disorders include hypoglycaemia (low blood sugars), liver shunt, hip and eye disorders – ask to see the breeder's health certificates for this last issue. A healthy Yorkie is long-lived with a lifespan of over 12 years.

SUMMARY: A sparky little companion akin to a Terrier. Suitable for the elderly and a possibility for allergy sufferers, but not recommended for families with small children. Pick one from a bloodline with a history of even temperaments.

West Highland White Terrier

Scottish white terriers were recorded during the 16th century reign of King James VI of Scotland (1567-1625), who ordered a dozen terriers to be brought from Argyll, western Scotland, and presented as a gift to France.

Sandy and brindle dogs were thought to be hardier than those of other colours; white dogs were seen as weak. At various times, the Westie has been considered a white offshoot of both the Scottish Terrier (which is black) and the sandy coloured Cairn Terrier.

In 1588 a Spanish Armada ship carrying white Spanish dogs was wrecked off the Isle of Skye. Descendants of the survivors were kept separate from other breeds by Clan Donald. Other Skye families, including Clan MacLeod, preserved both white and sandy coloured dogs, It was recorded that at least two Clan chiefs kept white terriers, including "The Wicked Man," Norman MacLeod (1705-1772), 22nd Chief of Clan MacLeod.

The little-known Poltalloch Terriers and Pittenweem Terriers are thought to be the Westie's ancestors. Edward Donald Malcolm (1837-1930), 16th Laird of Poltalloch, is the man who is credited with developing the modern Westie. He hunted game and the story goes that after a reddish-brown Terrier was mistaken for a fox and shot, he decided to develop a white Terrier which became known as the 'Poltalloch Terrier'. The first generation of Poltallochs had sandy coloured coats and the trademark pricked ears. The name West Highland White Terrier first appeared in 1908.

Today the Westie is one of the most popular Terriers on both sides of the Atlantic, but particularly in the UK. He is classed in the Terrier Group and has a strong prey instinct, but is often easier to train and handle than some Terriers. The American Kennel Club says the breed is: "known for its friendly, strong-willed personality and a remarkably bright white coat. Said to be "all terrier," this breed possesses a large amount of spunk, determination and devotion stuffed into a compact little body. The confident Westie excels in a variety of AKC events, from conformation to agility to obedience."

The Kennel Club (UK) says: "The West Highland White has a cheerful, outgoing personality. He makes an ideal companion and playmate for youngsters as he is full of fun and virtually tireless. He is always ready for a walk come snow or shine, and is small enough to pick up and take anywhere. The right size for house or flat, he really is an all-purpose pet."

The Westie is ranked 47th in the Intelligence of dogs, in the Average Working/Obedience Intelligence section. The Westie does, however, respond well to training as he's motivated by food, and indeed is a better dog with a confident owner. A lack of leadership can lead to issues such as biting and possessiveness over food and even furniture. A Westie with an owner who shows firm, consistent leadership is a much happier dog and one less likely to develop 'Small Dog Syndrome'.

The temperament of this game little dog can vary; some are very child-friendly, while others prefer more solitude. But generally, the Westie has a cheerful personality and loves people, making an affectionate addition to any household. Like all Terriers, he is tenacious rather than laid-back. Typically the breed is independent, assured and self-confident.

The AKC says that the Westie should be "possessed with no small amount of self-esteem" and generally this dog will NOT tolerate rough handling, such as a youngster tugging at its fur, tail or ears. This faithful companion generally travels well.

Like all Terriers, Westies make good watch dogs and will bark when someone knocks at the door, only too happy to greet them with a wagging tail or roll on their back for their tummy to be tickled by someone new.

They also live more happily alongside other dogs compared with some other Terrier breeds and are less aggressive towards strange dogs – although they may boss some dogs around! For a small dog, a Westie needs a fair amount of exercise - the Kennel Club recommends up to an hour a day. An under-exercised Westie can find plenty of mischief - including digging, barking and over-possessiveness.

A Westie's paws are slightly turned out to give the dog a better grip over rocky surfaces. In young puppies, the nose and paw pads are pink and slowly turn black. The white coat combines a soft dense undercoat with a rough outer coat.

Daily brushing and regular clipping or stripping of the coat is necessary, and unless you can do this yourself, you'll have to pay for trips to the groomers every couple of months or so. The Westie is considered a hypoallergenic dog and so may be suitable for some allergy sufferers.

The breed is in Category 2 of Breed Watch, with points of concern listed as "Misplaced lower canine teeth and skin irritation". In fact, skin issues with Westies are well documented. Atopic dermatitis – which is hereditary - is the number one health issue reported by owners, affecting one in four dogs, followed by luxating patella, bowel disease and Legg-Calvé-Perthes Disease (a hip condition).

The American breed club puts the lifespan at 12 to 16 years, another survey says 11.4 years, while data from UK vet clinics shows an average lifespan of 10.5 to 15 years.

SUMMARY: An affectionate and lively dog for the right owner who is prepared to spend time training. Choose a puppy with even-tempered parents with no history of skin problems.

Border Collie

The herding sheepdog, or shepherd's dog, has probably been around in Britain since Neolithic times, which ended 4,000 years ago. During this period Man began to farm and he domesticated sheep, goats and dogs. The term 'shepherd's dog' was used to describe any canine which worked with sheep.

By the 18th century, this type of dog had become a necessity in Scotland, as sheep played an increasingly important role in the country's economy. The breed's name comes from its likely place of origin along the Anglo-Scottish border. Mention of the 'Collie' or 'Colley' first appeared in the late 19th century, although the word is older, thought to come from the old Celtic word for useful.

In Australia, New Zealand and parts of the US where there are still huge flocks of sheep, specialised types of sheepdogs have developed and are still used - heelers, barkers and dogs capable of going over the backs of closely packed sheep or driving them long distances. But in Britain and in parts of the US, the Border Collie has emerged as the dominant herding dog.

Many of the best Border Collies today can be traced back to a dog called Old Hemp (1893-1903), who sired over 200 puppies. He was bred by Adam Telfer, a Northumberland farmer who was not only a shepherd, but a breeder and great sheepdog trainer. Old Hemp isn't number one in the International Sheep Dog Society stud book as he was added after the book began.

The Border Collie is in the Pastoral Group in the UK and Herding Group in the USA. According to the Intelligence of Dogs List, this breed is the brainiest on the planet; numero uno. No other canine can match him for the speed at which he learns commands and then carries them out, as anyone who has seen a shepherd training a young Border Collie will testify. It's not unusual for a dog to learn a new command in a few minutes with only a few repetitions.

This hardy dog was bred for hill conditions and is outstanding when it comes to working sheep. Unlike specialists of the past, the Border Collie is able to perform a variety of tasks, and the defining traits of the breed are the silent use of the concentrated stare, or 'eye,' to control the sheep, the crouching creep and the wide-circling outrun to gather the flock.

The Border Collie's good looks and ferocious intelligence has led to it becoming very popular. Unfortunately, the dog has become a victim of its own success and many hundreds have ended up in rescue centres after the owners are unable to cope with their obsessive behaviour when under-exercised or under-stimulated.

This is not a dog that can ever be happy sitting at home all day, and if he doesn't get the daily hours of exercise he needs, then poor or destructive behaviour can result. This breed should only be considered by farmers, owners who live a predominantly outdoor life, or those who are prepared for several hours of outdoor exercise on a regular basis – hiking, biking, jogging or canine activity contests. This dog is a workaholic, has a low boredom threshold and extremely high energy levels.

While the Border Collie is undoubtedly loyal and loving and bonds quickly with the right owner, he requires continual stimulation - mentally, emotionally and physically - much more than the average dog. In fact, many Border Collie experts say that the breed does NOT make a great family pet.

If Collies don't have a job, they will find one. They may give you the 'eye,' watching you constantly, as if you were a sheep, and then rush in front of you if they think something is going to happen. They may chase and nip anything that moves to keep themselves busy - this may include passing traffic, other animals, you, and small children in particular. A bored Collie often exhibits obsessive behaviour, such as chasing lights, shadows or running water, or barking excessively at an object, animal or person.

A Border Collie has been bred to work all day ... and then the day after and the day after that. A long walk at weekend isn't going to satisfy him. This breed needs as much exercise as he can get, ideally several hours a day. He loves to fetch balls or sticks and absolutely excels at any canine activity ever invented. Their greatest desire is to please you with their actions and they like to go everywhere with you – even if this means sitting in the car or truck sometimes. A second active dog helps to keep the Border Collie amused and exercised - but then you have double the cost and responsibility.

Some can be highly sensitive – to emotions, noise etc - and all should be well socialised with other dogs when young to prevent them becoming too timid. The breed is affectionate with those it knows and trusts, but can be wary of strangers.

The Border Collie is physically hardy - many farmers keep them outside in kennels - and has a dense, weather-resistant double coat which sheds a lot, making them unsuitable for allergy sufferers. There are two types of coat: long and smooth, which is shorter. Many Border Collies are black and white, but a number of colours are permitted by the Kennel Clubs. The bred is hardy and healthy, being in Breed Watch Category 1, no major points of concern. Hip dysplasia, Collie eye anomaly (CEA) and epilepsy are the main hereditary diseases.

SUMMARY: An exceptional working dog for a farmer or active outdoorsy owner. However, this instinctive canine can be extremely challenging without enough exercise and entertainment. If you haven't got a few hours a day to exercise this dog, consider a less demanding breed.

Doberman Pinscher

We have a German tax collector to thank for this breed. The Doberman Pinscher, which is simply called the Dobermann in the UK, is unique as it is the result of specific breedings to produce anticipated characteristics in a protection dog. In other words, the purpose for this dog was determined before the breed existed. The Dobermann is the only breed known to have been developed for this purpose.

Herr Karl Friedrich Louis Dobermann was born in 1834 in Thuringia, Germany. He ran the local dog pound and worked as a tax collector by day and a police officer at night. He wanted a protection dog that was strong, agile, intelligent, loyal and fearless; such a dog did not exist in Germany at that time.

In 1880, Herr Dobermann began his breeding programme with Thuringian Shepherds (ancestors of the German Shepherd Dog), early Rottweilers and German Shepherds. He visited dog shows and breeding kennels to find the characteristics he wanted. German Pinschers, Black and Tan Terriers, Weimaraners, Greyhounds and German Shorthaired

Pointers are all thought to have contributed to his early breed stock. Years of trial and error went by before the breed capable of reproducing itself now known as the Doberman Pinscher emerged.

After Dobermann's death in 1894, the Germans named the breed Dobermann-pinscher in his honour, but 50 years later dropped the 'pinscher' on the grounds that this German word for Terrier was no longer appropriate. The British did the same a few years later. During World War II, the United States Marine Corps adopted the Doberman Pinscher as its official War Dog, although the Corps also used other breeds in the role.

Dobermanns were originally known for being ferocious and aggressive. As a personal protection dog they had to be big, bold and intimidating, but obedient enough to do so only on command. These traits served the dog well in its role as a personal protection dog or police dog, but were not ideal for a companion. In fact over the decades, the breed's aggression has been much toned down by modern breeders.

Today's Dobermanns are far more even tempered and good natured, some are even therapy dogs. They are very loyal, highly intelligent and easy to train, making them much more desirable as a house dog. They are ranked at number five in the Intelligent of Dogs List, being one of the brightest of all the dog breeds. A typical Dobermann is also energetic, bold, watchful and obedient.

A Doberman has a keen sense of hearing and is extremely alert, making him an excellent watch dog and guard dog - the very sight of him barking is enough to deter most intruders. In the US, the ears and tail are often cropped, although this is illegal in Europe. With his powerful physique, sleek coat and clean lines, the Dobermann is striking - one reason why he is one of the most popular breeds in the USA. Less so in the UK, possibly due in some part to the fact that houses and gardens are smaller, the breed is growing in popularity.

The Kennel Club says: "The Dobermann has a very adaptable outlook to life and fits into a family well, playing with and guarding children. He enjoys riding in a car, and will take over the most comfortable chair in the house without even a second thought. He makes an excellent obedience dog."

With so many good traits, what's the downside of a Dobermann? Well, the main point is that these are extremely muscular and energetic dogs, particularly when young, and need a great deal of exercise – over two hours a day is recommended. They excel at mental and physical challenges, such as tracking, agility, Schutzhund and advanced obedience, and are a good choice if you are looking for a fitness partner when you hike, jog or cycle.

Dobermans are big chewers, especially when puppies or when not getting enough exercise. My friend's dog Jingo has chewed the sofa, carpet, wall, skirting boards and numerous shoes and gloves (in fact he completely ate the gloves), the only thing he hasn't chewed is the window sill. Crate training can be useful until a young dog learns not to chew.

They do not tolerate cold and are not suited to life outdoors, as they thrive on contact with humans - although they are not as needy as some breeds. They need a firm hand when training to learn that the human is the leader and they are the follower. Respect and protect are the bywords. Early socialisation with other dogs, people and children is essential, as under-socialised Dobermanns can be aggressive. From puppyhood they should be taught to walk calmly on a lead and not pull. These are extremely powerful dogs and you don't want to get into a strength contest or battle of wills with a fully-grown Dobermann.

The low-maintenance coat is short and smooth, but sheds a little and so the breed is not one for allergy sufferers. Almost all Dobermanns are black and tan, but can also be brown, blue or fawn with rust-red markings.

In Breed Watch Category 1, there are no major points of concern and average lifespan is 10 to 11 years. However, there are a number of health issues which can shorten a dog's life. Dilated cardiomyopathy (DCM or enlarged heart) can lead to sudden death and is a major problem within the breed. According to UFAW (Universities Federation for Animal Welfare), some 58% of all Dobermanns in Europe are affected. Breeding stock can be screened for the DCM gene with a blood test.

SUMMARY: A striking companion for energetic owners. Dominancy levels vary within litters, choose a pup which is not too dominant, as he will be less wilful and easier to train. Ensure the parents have been screened for DCM.

German Shorthaired Pointer

The German Shorthaired Pointer is a handsome and athletic dog which, as the name suggests, was developed in Germany as a versatile hunting dog. It is classed in the Gundog Group in the UK and Sporting Group in the USA.

Not a great deal is known about the exact origins of this highly intelligent and trainable breed, which is becoming more popular with hunt and canine activity fans in both the UK and North America.

It is thought that the GSP was developed in Germany in the late 1800s to be an all-purpose hunting dog capable of carrying out a number of different tasks in the field, while being relatively easy to train.

According to the AKC, its ancestors were probably a breed known as the German Bird Dog, related to the old Spanish Pointer introduced to Germany in the 17th century. It is also likely that various German hound and tracking dogs, as well as the English Pointer and the Arkwright Pointer, also contributed to the development of the breed. As the first studbook was not created until 1870, it is impossible to identify all of the dog's ancestors. The breed was officially recognised by the AKC in 1930.

The GSP was bred to point, retrieve, track wounded game, hunt both large and small game - fur and feather - and to work in deep cover as well as in water. He was also intended to be a family companion, and is good with both adults and children. By temperament the typical GSP is highly active – as are most dogs bred to work – and requires at least two hours of exercise off the lead every day. He is ideally suited to sportsmen and women or active, ourdoorsy owners who want a dog they can take anywhere and who can give the dog the exercise he needs to be happy.

The selective breeding to produce the German Shorthaired Pointer has resulted in a highly intelligent dog, listed at number seventeen in the 'Excellent Working Dogs' section of the Intelligence of Dogs. However, this intelligence, combined with the breed's independent-mindedness, can lead to problems if the dog is not properly trained. Many GSPs will ignore commands if they don't feel like obeying at that particular moment. They are scent hounds and easily distracted, setting off after an interesting scent or sight at the drop of a hat if not trained.

GSPs tend to be eager to please and training should start early with short, entertaining sessions. Even though some may appear physically mature at six months, their brain may not be engaged until they reach two years old, and you may find yourself with a child housed in the body of an adult dog. Pups and adolescents tend to be very bouncy and completely unaware of everything else, so guard your young children and prize ornaments if you don't want them to get knocked over in the excitement.

A German Shorthaired Pointer thrives on structure and leadership, and is easily biddable with the right owner who is prepared to put in the time at the beginning. Training teaches the dog not only obedience, but gives him the confidence to carry out the commands. Well-trained GSPs excel in so many fields, not only hunting, but also field trials, obedience and agility events, search and rescue, bomb and drug detection, and even as therapy dogs. This is a dog which thoroughly enjoys to work.

The other stand-out feature of this striking breed is its unwavering loyalty to, and affection for, its humans. GSPs are very centred on their owners, and sometimes even referred to as 'Velcro' dogs, as they can be very clingy. They are not suitable to be left alone for hours on end every day, and neither should they be kept outside in a kennel. They need to be living as companions within the family home. When lonely, they can lose confidence and become nervous or destructive or bark a lot. Although these are even tempered and good natured dogs, they can sometimes be mischievous – and will certainly make you laugh from time to time.

GSPs are not generally aggressive with other dogs or people. They can be reserved with strangers and make good watch dogs. They should, however, be socialised with other dogs when young, as some can show aggression towards strange dogs. They have an instinct to hunt, so if you have a cat, introduce them while the dog is still a pup.

Physically, the GSP is sleek and elegant yet powerful and muscular, appearing to possess every physical attribute a dog could ever wish for. The UK Kennel Club says: "Noble, steady dog showing power, endurance and speed, giving the immediate impression of an alert and energetic dog whose movements are well co-ordinated."

The breed is clean to keep and has a short, easy to maintain coat which sheds a little, making it unsuitable for allergy sufferers. The coat can be liver, liver and white, solid black or black and white; it may be spotted or ticked or both. Like all breeds with floppy ears, the GSP is prone to infections and regular ear cleaning should be a part of normal grooming. In the UK and Europe the tail is left natural unless working, in the USA the tail is docked to around half length.

This is a generally healthy breed which stays fit well into old age. It is listed in Breed Watch Category 1 with no major points of concern and has a typical lifespan of 12 to 14 years. A UK survey put the median age at 12 years, with one dog living 17 years. Health issues include hip dysplasia – ask to see screening certificates – heart, eye and skin disorders.

SUMMARY: A handsome and athletic working dog suitable for active owners and those with an interest in canine activities.

Jack Russell Terrier

The Jack Russell Terrier is the only breed in this list not recognised by the Kennel Clubs. KC and AKC recognition for the Jack Russell has been opposed by the breed's societies – which has resulted in the breeding and recognition of the not dissimilar Parson Russell Terrier.

The reason is outlined by the Jack Russell Club of America: "Jack Russell Terriers are a type, or strain, of working terrier; they are not pure bred in the sense that they have a broad genetic make-up, a broad standard, and do not breed true to type. This is a result of having been bred strictly for hunting since their beginning in the early 1800s, and their preservation as a working breed since.

"The broad standard, varied genetic background based on years of restricted inbreeding and wide out crossing, and great variety of size and type, are the major characteristics that make this strain of terrier known as a Jack Russell such a unique, versatile working terrier."

The Jack Russell Terrier was developed by the Reverend John Russell (known as Jack), from Devon, England, in the mid-to-late 1800s.

He enjoyed hunting foxes, a popular pastime with Victorian clergymen, and was a keen breeder of foxhunting dogs. He bought a small white and tan female called Trump from a milkman and started a breeding programme to develop a Terrier with enough stamina for the hunt as well as the courage and body shape suitable to pursue foxes that had gone to ground. It is thought that the JRT and the Fox Terrier share common ancestors.

If you sliced a Jack Russell in two (heaven forbid!), you would find the word 'Terrier' stamped though him, like a stick of seaside rock. He has the high energy levels of a Fox Terrier, the hardiness and working stamina of a Border Terrier, and is as cocky and tenacious as a Yorkshire Terrier. He has a very strong prey drive and great determination and intensity.

A Jack Russell Terrier approaches life full on and is not for the faint hearted. If you want a quiet life, then don't get a Jack Russell. On the other hand, if you ride horses and want a dog to run alongside, or enjoy walking in the countryside every day, then this lively Terrier with the big personality could be just the dog for you. Some time ago we looked after a Jack Russell called Butch at the same time as Gus, a German Shepherd, for several weeks. The dogs got on pretty well together, despite them both being males and elderly, but there was no doubt who the boss was – and it wasn't Gus.

The Jack Russell is feisty and quite vociferous, they love to bark at new people and things, although are often friendly towards strangers. When he's not barking, two of his other favourite hobbies are digging and chewing, especially when as a pup and adolescent.

Their temperament has not changed much over the last 160 years or so. This is why the Jack Russell Terrier breed societies didn't want their dog recognised by the Kennel Clubs. They don't want the breed to have to conform to an exacting physical appearance, like pedigree dogs, where the look of the dog is all-important. In contrast, the JRT has been bred specifically to do a job, and that is the most important aspect of this little Terrier.

The Jack Russell Terrier Club of Great Britain (JRTCGB) says: "The terrier must present a lively, active and alert appearance. It should impress with its fearless and happy disposition. It should be remembered that the Jack Russell is a working terrier and should retain these instincts. Nervousness, cowardice and over-aggression should be discouraged, and it should always appear confident.

"A sturdy, tough terrier, very much on its toes all the time, measuring between 10" and 15" at the withers. The body length must be in proportion to the height, and it should present a compact, balanced image, always being in solid, hard condition."

The dog's appearance may vary. He can have a smooth coat, a rough coat or a combination of the two. The height of the breed varies considerably from around eight inches high at the withers (shoulders) to about 12 inches high (taller in the USA). Over half the body should be covered in white with black, brown and/or tan markings or, typically, patches.

The Jack Russell Terrier and the Parson Russell Terrier are similar and share a common origin, but they have several marked differences — the most notable being the range of acceptable heights. Parson Russells generally have longer legs, a bigger body and longer head, and they are taller, ranging from 12 to 14 inches in height.

Jack Russells are clever, active dogs which like to spend time (but not live) outside. Pound for pound, the breed's energy levels are extremely high, and they are not generally suitable for apartment life or as a companion for the elderly - although older dogs are less active. Nor are they hypoallergenic; their coat is low maintenance, but they still shed hair. Sadly too many JRTs finish up in rescue centres, as prospective owners fall for their cute looks, not realising that this is a physically active and demanding dog that requires time-consuming obedience training, socialisation and a daily hour of exercise to be content, preferably running free. The breed loves farms and large gardens and will generally show the typical Terrier trait of chasing cats, squirrels and other small creatures unless they have been introduced to them at a young age.

An indicator to the fearless and active nature of these dogs can be gained from the fact that show dogs can be accepted with scars. JRTCGB states: "Old scars or injuries, the result of work or accident, should not be allowed to prejudice the terrier's chance in the show ring unless they interfere with its movement or with its utility for work or stud."

Jack Russells are relatively easy to train, they love learning tricks and do well in canine competitions. Socialisation and obedience training from puppyhood is important to prevent them showing aggression to other animals and people and barking at the drop of a hat. Puppy classes are an excellent way to start training with a JRT. In short, they are super, feisty little dogs, but only for the right home where owners have the time and desire to train, exercise, play with and supervise this fun little bundle of energy. JRTs definitely don't like being left for long periods and can become destructive or noisy when lonely.

The breed has a reputation for being healthy with a long lifespan of 13 to 16 years. Some bloodlines have shown problems with cataracts, deafness and patellar luxation; ask the breeder if the parents or grandparents have any history of these issues.

Although the breed is not registered with the Kennel Club, you can find responsible breeders through The Jack Russell Terrier Club of Great Britain at www.jrtcgb.co.uk or the Jack Russell Terrier Club of America at www.therealjackrussell.com. The breed clubs also maintain a register of Jack Russell Terriers. The image below shows a smooth coated Jack Russell Terrier (left) and a Parson Russell Terrier.

4. Crossbreed or Mixed Breed?

If you get a purebred dog, you have a good idea of how the dog will turn out physically, what it was originally bred for and what its natural instincts will be. But not everybody wants a pedigree dog.

Pedigree breeders select their dams and sires based on a number of attributes, but over the years inherent faults have sometimes been inadvertently passed on through the bloodlines along with all the good points. For example, some Dalmatians are deaf, some Labradors have hip problems and Dachshunds may suffer from back problems.

Because specific dogs within the breed were selected for mating, the gene pool of a pedigree is likely to be narrower than that of a mixed breed or mongrel. It is said that all Cavalier King Charles Spaniels can trace their ancestry back to six dogs.

Some people believe that a crossbreed (also called a hybrid) or mongrel will be naturally healthier than a pedigree dog, which may have inheritable weaknesses. However, it is worth bearing in mind that two unhealthy crossbreeds or mongrels will not necessarily produce healthy puppies, so picking a good breeder and looking at the health and temperament of the parents (the puppy's, not the breeder's!) applies just as much, if not even more so with a crossbreed.

There is much discussion on something called hybrid vigour, which is one reason why some people choose to get a crossbreed dog. This is the tendency of a cross-bred individual to show qualities superior to those of both parents.

Hybrid Vigour

According to scientists, hybrid vigour (heterosis) is: "The increased vigour displayed by the offspring from a cross between genetically different parents.

"Hybrids from crosses between different crop varieties (F1 hybrids) are often stronger and produce better yields than the original varieties. Mules, the offspring of mares crossed with donkeys, have greater strength and resistance to disease and a longer lifespan than either parent."

Hybrid vigour applies to plants and animals.

Cockapoos, Labradoodles, Goldendoodles, Schnoodles, all the Poos and Doodles and other so-called 'designer dogs' are causing a big debate. The hybrid vigour theory as it applies to the canine world is that a crossbred puppy may be stronger and healthier than a purebred, as he or she is less likely to inherit the genetic faults of either purebred parent.

For example, one parent dog could be blind with PRA, the other suffering from Von Willebrands disease and the offspring would be carriers, but perfectly healthy as long as they don't share the diseases in common. A Labrador with hip dysplasia mated to a Poodle with luxating patellas will almost certainly produce normal offspring, but – and this is a big but - **hybrid vigour declines in successive generations.**

So, taking the above example, a first generation puppy (F1) with a pedigree Labrador and pedigree Poodle for parents will almost certainly be healthy, but a second generation puppy (F2), such as a puppy with two Labradoodle parents, will naturally carry a much higher chance of suffering from or carrying the gene for PRA or hip dysplasia.

Of course, responsible breeders of crossbreed puppies should also be taking this into account, just as good pedigree breeders do, when selecting their breeding pairs.

Because crossbreed and mongrels are not pedigree dogs, you cannot get Kennel Clubs or AKC registration papers with your dog. But despite this, you should always find out about your dog's parents and ancestry – because provided you care for him well, his genes will be the major factor in deciding how healthy he will be. Also, some crossbreed societies keep registration details of puppies from recognised breeders.

F Numbers

If you are considering a crossbreed dog, then you need to understand just what you are getting – and the breeders' terminology involves F numbers, which have nothing at all to do with Formula 1 racing or camera lenses! F stands for filial; it comes from the Latin *filius* (son) and means "relating to a son or daughter."

A first generation **(F1)** crossbreed is one where both parents are pedigree dogs. The next generations are worked out by always adding one number up from the lowest number parent.

An **F2** could be the offspring of two F1 dogs or the product of an F1 dog crossed with an F2 or F3 or F4.

An **F3** is the offspring of one F2 parent where the other was F2 or higher, for example: an F2 crossed with an F3 or F2 or F4.

Then it gets even more complicated in some cases with F1B, F2B, F3B, and so on crosses. The B stands for Backcross. This occurs when a litter has been produced as a result of a backcross to one of the parent breeds – often a Poodle to produce a more consistent coat - so this could be a Goldendoodle bred with a Poodle. It is not common practice for breeders to backcross to the non-shedding breed, in this case a Golden Retriever. So a typical F1B might be one quarter Golden Retriever (or Labrador in the case of Labradoodles or Cocker Spaniel in the case of Cockapoos) and three-quarters   Poodle.

Sticking with Goldendoodles, a second generation backcross pup (F2B) is the result of an F1 Goldendoodle bred to a Goldendoodle backcross (F1B). Although three generations in the making, F2Bs are technically second generation dogs.

All clear?? Well, we're moving on anyway! With Labradoodles (and several other crosses) there is also such a thing as a **multigeneration or multigen** Labradoodle, which is the result of successive Labradoodle to Labradoodle breeding, rather than breeding purebred Labradors and Poodles. However, in practice, backcrosses and Poodles are also used in the early generations. This is why some older lines of multigeneration Labradoodles have a lot of Poodle in their genetic make-up.

Poodles are less expensive and, as they have a wool coat, increase the likelihood of the puppies having a low-shed or non-shedding coat. They also introduce some popular new colours such as red and parti (white and another colour). Hybrid vigour may be lost, but the advantage of

multigens is that good breeders can reproduce a more consistent size, appearance and coat type by breeding multigen to multigen.

NOTE: All Australian Labradoodles are multigeneration, but not all multigenerations are Australian Labradoodles.

The main point to remember with the Poodle crossbreeds is that none of them is guaranteed to be non-shedding or hypoallergenic. You need to spend time with the individual dog before you can be 100% sure.

Today there are literally dozens and dozens of crossbreeds, far too many to mention here. You may be going for a particular cross because you like the look of the dog, if so then check out the health records and temperaments of the parents as well as just how the dogs look.

If you are selecting a crossbreed because you have allergies, it is also worth considering a hypoallergenic pedigree breed, and even then you have to spend time with the individual dog. Some responsible hybrid breeders will not sell to families or individuals who are selecting their puppies purely because they have allergies. Allergies are so individual that there is no guarantee from one person to the next and one puppy to the next – and they don't want to risk their puppies going to unsuitable homes.

This is what the website VetStreet has to say: "Opening your heart and home to a crossbreed is like opening a beautifully wrapped package on your birthday: you can never be sure what's inside.

"It's often assumed that a crossbreed will combine the best of two or more breeds, but genetics doesn't always work that way. The way genes express themselves is not always subject to a breeder's control, even less so when two different breeds are crossed.

"That's something to keep in mind before you lay down lots of money for a dog that you have been assured will be hypoallergenic or healthier than a purebred."

Six Key Tips When Selecting A Crossbreed

If you decide to get a pedigree dog, you can be pretty sure of several factors:

- ❖ Which Kennel Club group the breed is in
- ❖ What the breed was originally developed for
- ❖ The natural instincts of this breed, e.g. whether it is likely to chase cats and other small animals, whether the dog has a high work ethic and how the breed in general responds to training
- ❖ The typical temperament of the breed
- ❖ How big your puppy will grow
- ❖ What coat type it will have
- ❖ What health issues the breed is susceptible to

If you get a crossbreed, there are many more uncertainties as to how your puppy will turn out. Even puppies within the same litter will grow to different sizes, often have different coat types, and some even have a coat which changes after a few months. While all puppies are a mix of both parents, some will take on more characteristics from the father (or sire), while others will have more in common with the mother (dam). When the father and mother are from different breeds, this enormously increases the possible variations of how your pup will look and act as an adult dog.

All the dogs pictured above are Schnoodles yet, as you can see, they vary tremendously in size, colour, coat and probably temperament too. None, one, some or all may be hypoallergenic, but there is no guarantee. The Kennel Clubs say that crossbreeds don't 'breed true', meaning that the puppies don't display a consistent set of characteristics.

Some breeders of hybrids breed multigeneration dogs, such as the Australian Labradoodle, which is Australian Labradoodle bred with an Australian Labradoodle. The advantage of this is that they produce a more consistent puppy; the disadvantage is that any hybrid vigour is lost.

Here are our Top Tips to help you make the right decision when selecting a crossbreed to help steer you towards a healthy puppy with the attributes you are looking for:

1. If hybrid vigour is one reason you are choosing a crossbred dog over a purebred dog, pick a first generation (F1) cross. Hybrid vigour decreases with each successive generation.

2. Research both of the parent breeds. For example, if you are interested in Goldendoodles, read about Poodles and Labradoodles, your puppy will be a combination of these breeds.

3. Go on the internet and look up the breed societies or associations for the crossbreed you are interested in - virtually all hybrids have them. The societies lay down a code of ethics for breeders and many also state how the dog should look and what sort of temperament it should ideally have.

4. Select an approved or recommended breeder. This is especially important with crossbreeds, which are not regulated by the Kennel Clubs. Anybody can take two dogs off the street, allow them to mate and call their puppies "designer dogs". With puppies fetching hundreds and even thousands of pounds or dollars, a lot of unscrupulous people have been tempted into the "designer dog" breeding game. The crossbreed societies have lists of breeders who conform to their standards.

5. Once you have chosen your breeder, read **Chapter 7.** on how to select the temperament of the puppy. For example, you might be interested in a Puggle, a cross between a Pug, which is affectionate and loving, and a Beagle, which is more independent-minded. Do the PAT test to see if the pup is more likely to take after the Pug or the Beagle.

6. Research the health problems of the parent breeds. Ask the breeder if he or she screens the breeding pair for these disorders and ask to see the certificates. Three of the most common hereditary ailments are eye and hip or elbow conditions, all of which can be screened for.

Now we'll take a look at some of the most popular crossbreed dogs.

Cockapoo

The Cockapoo, Cockerpoo, Cock-A-Poo or Spoodle is a cross between a Cocker Spaniel (English or American) and any size of Poodle. This is probably the number one crossbreed in the UK and extremely popular in North America. The Cockapoo is one of the oldest so-called "designer crossbreeds" having originated in the US from the early 1960s or even late 1950s.

This crossbreed's popularity is largely due to the fact that not only are they extremely cute, but they are known for having the friendly, outgoing and non-aggressive temperament of the Cocker, coupled with characteristics from the Poodle's non-shedding coat.

That's not to say that Cockapoos don't shed – most do, but nowhere near as much as a Spaniel and most types have low dander coats.

According to the Cockapoo Club of Great Britain: "The coat type of the Cockapoo will vary as characteristics are inherited from both the Poodle and the Cocker Spaniel. There may even be some variety within a litter.

"The three possible coat types are a tight curly coat, a loose wavy/ringlet coat and a straighter coat. An experienced breeder will be able to advise you what the likely coat type of a puppy will be from their Cocker Spaniel/Poodle mix that they breed, and when the puppies are just a few weeks old it is possible to see the coat type starting to develop.

"The texture of the Cockapoo coat usually consists of dense, soft or silky fur, unlike the coarser fur found on many dogs, and all three coat types of the F1 Cockapoo will be low-shedding/dander with low-allergen qualities."

NOTE: These are generally low shedding dogs, not non-shedding dogs. A Cockapoo may be suitable for some allergy sufferers, but it is by no means guaranteed.

The Cockapoo Club adds: "The Cockapoo bred back to a Poodle, the F1b, is more likely to have a tight curly coat as there is more of the Poodle in the gene pool. Similarly, the Cockapoo bred back to a Cocker Spaniel may have a straighter coat. The curlier coat types are generally less likely to shed any hair."

Cockapoos can be groomed to look like a Poodle or a Spaniel; you can also keep them in a puppy clip with the body coat trimmed to a short, fluffy length, with the hair on the legs left a little fuller and the tail left long and plume-like. Some owners learn to use clippers themselves, but most rely on trips to a professional dog groomers every couple of months – another cost to consider.

In between, Cockapoos are high maintenance on the grooming front. They need daily or near-daily brushing to prevent matting, as well as regular baths to keep them clean. Neglecting grooming can soon lead to a matted mess that can lead to painful skin infections. Like all Spaniels, a Cockapoo's ears should be kept clean and dry and regularly checked for any sign of infection. If you notice a nasty smell, redness or swelling, the ear has become infected and it's time to visit your vet. Also, Cockapoos commonly develop reddish-brown tear stains beneath their eyes, so regular washing of the face and careful wiping beneath the eyes should also be part of your regular grooming regime.

The colour varies a great deal, it can be: black, tan, beige, or buff, red - including auburn and apricot – light to dark brown, sable, cream, white, silver, brindle, roan or merle (mottled). Cockapoos can be one solid colour or have complex markings; they can be white with patches of any colour or have spots or freckles of colour, called ticking.

The well-trained and socialised Cockapoo has a sweet temperament, is friendly with people and is generally happy-go-lucky. He is also quite robust. However, be prepared for lots of exercise, many have high energy levels – higher than some people realise. This should not be a surprise to anyone, since both Spaniels and the original Poodles were bred as working dogs.

Make sure to ask the breeder whether the Cockapoo puppy you are looking at has been bred from working or show (conformation) lines. If you are looking for a more placid Cockapoo with lower energy levels, go for one bred from show stock and check out the parents - are they hyper or placid? Your pup will take after the parents. It is very difficult to tire out a Cockapoo bred from working lines. Cockapoos are, however, normally very biddable and easy to train.

Cockapoos, just like pedigree dogs, can suffer from health issues. One of the main ones is eye disorders, including progressive retinal atrophy (PRA). The Cockapoo clubs on both sides of the Atlantic strongly recommend testing breeding stock for this – ask to see CERF (USA) or CCGB certificates in the UK. Other issues include luxating patella, hip dysplasia and von Willebrands disease. Cockapoos are generally long lived, with 12 to 15 years being the norm.

If a breeder tells you the tests aren't necessary because (s)he's never had any problems in his or her lines, that the dogs have been "vet checked," or gives any other excuse for skimping on the genetic testing of their dogs, walk away. The Cockapoo's popularity has led to puppy farms and backyard breeders springing up with the main aim of making money from the craze – without paying too much attention to the long-term health and temperament of the puppies they produce, or the welfare of their breeding dogs.

VetStreet says: "Cockapoos who are carefully bred and lovingly raised should be happy, affectionate dogs that love families, children, other dogs, and even cats. Without the benefit of health and temperament testing, however, they can be a mess of genetic and behavioral problems."

There are, however, Cockapoo clubs in North America and the UK which are working towards developing the Cockapoo by breeding successive generations and establishing it as a recognised breed. The Cockapoo Club of GB promotes "Open and Ethical Breeding to Protect the Cockapoo of Tomorrow, Today."

These societies have registers for Cockapoos produced by approved breeders who agree to work to a Code of Ethics and have his or her dog's health tested. The first point of call for anyone interested in getting a Cockapoo should be one of these breed societies to find their list of approved breeders. Some useful links are: www.cockapooclubgb.co.uk, www.cockapooclub.com, and www.americancockapooclub.com.

SUMMARY: Friendly, affectionate, trainable and intelligent medium-sized dogs who like to be around people. They are often good with cats, children and other dogs and animals. Some have high energy levels and all need a lot of grooming. They are usually friendly with strangers, so they don't make good watchdogs. Many are low shedding.

Labradoodle

Since Wally Conron first crossed a Standard Poodle with a Labrador in 1988 and coined the phrase 'Labradoodle', this honest, sociable and fun-loving canine has made his home at the centre of families across the globe. Originating in Australia, the Labradoodle has become extremely popular elsewhere, particularly in the USA, Canada and the UK.

Wally worked as breeding manager for the Royal Guide Dog Association of Australia in Melbourne in the 1980s. He received a request from Pat Blum, a visually-impaired woman in Hawaii who had never applied for a guide dog before because of her husband's allergy to dogs, and who wrote to Wally in the hope that he might be able to help.

He had the novel idea of breeding a Labrador with a Standard Poodle with the goal of combining the low-shedding coat of the Poodle with the gentleness and trainability of the Labrador and ultimately produce a service/guide dog suitable for people with allergies to fur and dander.

The first three pups were Sultan, Sheik and Simon. Coat and saliva samples were flown to Pat in Hawaii, where it was discovered that her husband was allergic to two of the three but had no reaction to Sultan, who went on to live a happy life as Pat's guide dog in Hawaii.

The media hype and the fact that all Labradoodles have been promoted by some breeders as being perfectly suitable for all allergy sufferers has led to some criticism of the crossbreed, as well as a rash of puppy farms being set up by people looking to make a quick profit – but none of this is the fault of the dog.

To set the record straight, as the Kennel Clubs will tell anyone who asks, **there is no such thing as a totally non-shedding dog.** There are, however, certain breeds – and crossbreeds - which may be more suitable for allergy sufferers. Some MAY be suitable, but by no means all. If you suffer from allergies you need to spend time with the specific puppy.

Labradoodles come in three different sizes with three different coat types and many different colours. Miniatures weight 15 to 30lb, Mediums are 30 to 45lb, while Standards seems to be getting bigger every year and can weigh anything from 45 to more than 100lb.

A Labradoodle may be a first generation crossbreed, a second, third or fourth generation or a multigeneration, also called multigen. In extremely general terms, an F1 (first generation) Labradoodle has a scruffy look, while multigens and Australian Labradoodles look more like teddy bears. When you have decided what type of Labradoodle you'd like, you then have to decide what F number of dog you want - or whether to go for a multigen.

Whether Australian or simply Labradoodle, one reason why these dogs are so popular is their temperament, combining the placidity and steadfastness of the Labrador with the intelligence of the Poodle.

By nature Labradoodles are sociable, friendly, affectionate and non-aggressive with other dogs. They love to be with people and at the heart of family life and are therefore not suitable pets to be left alone all day. They are also intelligent, playful and highly trainable, but need plenty of mental and physical stimulation.

Standards are big dogs and can be boisterous and mischievous. Miniatures are becoming more popular, but still average around 18" in height. They want nothing more than to please their people and thrive on interaction. They enjoy a challenge, love games and are easily bored.

Most Labradoodles love water - and mud – so if you are particularly house proud, a smaller, less active breed might be a better choice. Labradoodles love to run, swim and fetch. Their energy levels vary greatly, so it's a good idea to try and see the parents, as puppies will generally take after them in this respect. They will bark if someone comes to the door, but are watch dogs rather than guard dogs, as they are likely to welcome any intruder with a wagging tail.

As with all dogs they should be treated with respect and given firm, fair training and handling from a very early age, or they will try to outsmart you. They often live happily with other dogs, cats and other animals, and usually do well with children. They do not like being left alone for long periods.

A Labradoodle can have one of three coats, and each type has variations. There are a large number of coat colours, including apricot/gold, red, black, silver, blue, caramel, chocolate, cafe, parchment and lavender. The three main coat types are:

Hair coat: also known as a flat or slick coat, although it may be straight or wavy, usually seen in F1 and other early generation Labradoodles. It is harsher in texture that wool or fleece and this coat normally sheds, so is not suitable for allergy sufferers.

Fleece coat: This is the coat that most people associate with an Australian Labradoodle and is also the one that requires most maintenance, requiring regular grooming to prevent matting. It should have no body odour and little to no shedding, although it is typical to find the occasional fur ball around the house. A fleece coat is acceptable for some people with allergies.

Wool coat: This is very dense and similar in texture to lambs' wool. It can be kept long, but that requires more grooming in this style. Kept short it is easy to maintain, has little or no doggie smell and minimal shedding. This coat is most like that of the Poodle and may be suitable for some allergy sufferers.

Health issues which can affect Labradoodles are similar to those affecting Labradors and Poodles. They include eye problems such as PRA (Progressive Retinal Atrophy) and hereditary cataracts, hip and elbow dysplasia, as well as Addison's disease in Australian Labradoodles.

Lifespan is anywhere from 10 to 15 years.

Useful contacts: UK - www.labradoodletrust.com, www.labradoodle.org.uk; USA - http://alaa-labradoodles.com, www.australianlabradoodleclub.us, http://labradoodle-dogs.net

---

Goldendoodle

The Goldendoodle is a cross between a Golden Retriever and a Poodle, usually a Standard or Miniature. They come in three sizes: Miniature (weighing 15 to 30lb), Medium (30 to 45lb) and Standard (45 to more than 100lb). On colour, they can be white, cream, apricot, gold, red, sometimes grey and black (phantom), black or a light sandy brown.

In the 1990s, breeders in both North America and Australia began crossing Golden Retrievers with Standard Poodles with the aim of developing guide dogs suitable for visually impaired individuals with allergies, similar to what Wally Conron had done with the Labradoodle years earlier.

Although not all Goldendoodles exhibit the non-shedding coat type of the Poodle, many have a low to non-shedding coat.

Often the Goldendoodle moults less than a Golden Retriever (which sheds a lot), but the degree varies from one dog to the next and grooming requirements vary with coat types. The coat length when left unclipped grows to about four to eight inches long.

As with Labradoodles, some breeders claim that the Goldendoodle is hypoallergenic, but this is simply not true as the variations within a crossbreed are greater than that within pedigree dogs and even puppies within the same litter may have different coats. Although it is true to say that some Goldendoodles are suitable for some allergy sufferers.

There are three main coat types: **straight**, which is flat and more like a Golden Retriever coat, **wavy** is a mixture of a Poodle's curls and a Golden Retriever's straighter fur, and **curly**, which is more like the Poodle coat.

The amount of grooming depends on the coat type – and if yours is low-shedding, you will have to factor in the cost of regular trims at the groomers every two or three months. In between, a Goldendoodle should be brushed at least every other day. As with many long-eared dogs, ear infections can be a problem. The ears should be kept dry and clean, especially after a bath or swimming; redness, a bad smell and head shaking are all signs of a potential infection, which needs dealing with promptly by a veterinarian.

The appearance of the Goldendoodle runs anywhere from shaggy Retriever to curly Poodle, but usually falls somewhere in between.

This crossbreed has become hugely popular in North America, where many owners describe it as a wonderful family pet which is sociable, intelligent, affectionate and easy to train. It often combines the outstanding temperament of the Golden Retriever - with its friendliness, affection and even-temperedness - with the intelligence and intuition of the Poodle.

Goldendoodles are usually very affectionate with people and other pets. They are human-oriented dogs, and tend to develop a strong bond with their owners and companions. They often have an uncanny ability to communicate with people. Most are calm and easy going, but they are active dogs that do require a fair amount of daily exercise. Generally they could be described as having moderate energy levels, although this varies from one individual to the next – check out the parents, - what are they like? Larger ones are often more active.

The Goldendoodle's Poodle and Labrador Retriever ancestors were hunters and water dogs. Some like to swim, but not all. They need a good walk or active playtime each day, and they are athletic enough to participate in such dog sports as agility, flyball, obedience and rally. They can also be excellent therapy dogs. They tend to be great family pets and are known to be especially good with children, being inclined to be careful around infants or toddlers, and can be great playmates for older children.

GANA (Goldendoodle Association of North America) has laid down a basis upon which the breed standard will be created for the Goldendoodle:
- ❖ A balanced mix of physical characteristics of the Golden Retriever and the Poodle
- ❖ A consistently friendly, social temperament similar to that of the Golden Retriever
- ❖ Consists of Poodle and Golden Retriever only - no other breed infusion is accepted
- ❖ No tail docking or body altering other than the removal of dew claws - dew claw removal is optional.

Many Goldendoodles are first generation (F1) crosses, and as such may be expected to benefit from hybrid vigour. However, Goldendoodles generally can be susceptible to the health problems of Golden Retrievers, Standard Poodles, or Miniature Poodles. These include eye and heart problems, hip dysplasia and Addison's disease. Ask the breeder to see both of the puppy's parents' certificates for eye and joint issues.

Like the Labradoodle, lifespan can vary from 10 to 15 years.

Contacts: http://www.goldendoodleassociation.com, http://goldendoodles.com

---

Puggle

A Puggle is a cross between two dogs which have seen a big rise in popularity recently – the Pug and the Beagle. And their offspring is rapidly becoming one of the most popular hybrid dogs of all time. This is slightly surprising as the breeders of Puggles, unlike the breeders of many other crossbreeds, make no claims to their dogs being hypoallergenic.

No, the appeal of the Puggle lies primarily in his personality, coupled with his other attributes of being a fairly small dog with moderate exercise and low grooming requirements.

As with many so-called "designer dogs", it all started in the USA. Wisconsin breeder Wallace Havens bred the first Puggle in the 1980s. He invented the name and was the first to register the breed with the American Canine Hybrid Club. By 2000, Puggles were being sold commercially.

At first glance, these two breeds might seem like an odd mix. Pugs are affectionate little homebodies. They are one of the brachycephalic (flat-faced) breeds and their short noses can make them less exercise-tolerant than other breeds the same size. This is an affectionate, stubborn, playful companion dog which loves nothing better than sitting on his owner's lap.

Beagles are great family dogs that can walk all day, but they are often ruled by their nose and can be escape artists and hard to lure back if they wander off. They also have a tendency to howl if they are bored or unhappy. The Beagle is altogether more independent minded and nowhere near as reliant upon humans for his happiness.

Indeed, the Beagle has a tendency to roam, and there is a saying if you want to find a Beagle owner in a park, it's the man with a lead looking for his dog! Beagles are scent hounds bred to track game and have an incredible sense of smell. They are sometimes called a nose on four legs, which is why they often wander off on the trail of an interesting scent.

Pugs and Beagles are both short-coated, small, cute and popular - and that's where the similarity ends! Bred skilfully you have the best of both worlds: a robust, healthy little dog with a playful spirit, a sense of humour and a desire to please. At best the Puggle can be a hardy little dog with the adventurous yet quieter spirit of a Beagle and the clever antics of a Pug. But you could end up with a puppy which has inherited the other traits: stubborn, exercise-intolerant, hard to train, uncooperative, not very attached to you and who will wander off at every opportunity.

Some unscrupulous people are making a lot of money out of breeding Puggles for profit, with no great interest in improving this crossbreed. Make sure you pick your breeder carefully, don't just fall for the first cute Puggle pup you clap eyes on – one thing all Puggle pups have in common is that they are ALL cute!

The importance of selecting the right breeder and then the right puppy cannot be stressed enough with Puggles. It's essential for you to visit the breeder's home, watch the puppies and look at the temperament of, ideally, both parents. If that's not possible, then spend some time with the mother to see if she has an affectionate temperament or if she is stand-offish. Look at the Pug parent, how flat is the nose? Does (s)he appear to be having difficulty breathing, is he or she snuffling or snorting a lot? If so, avoid a pup from this parent, go for a Puggle with a longer nose more like a Beagle.

And before you visit the breeder, read **Chapter 7. Picking the Individual Puppy** for some invaluable advice on choosing the right temperament to fit in with you and your family or household. With good breeding, the Pug's love of humans and home should balance the Beagle's independent ways and offset the little hound's tendency to be an escape artist and a roamer.

Puggles can be barkers if they take after the Beagle side, and this wants nipping in the bud when young. They usually get along with other dogs, but not always with cats, as the Beagle's chase instinct may predominate. Both Pugs and Beagles can have a stubborn streak, especially when it comes to training. Patience and treats are the answer – but not too many.

Both the Beagle and the Pug are notorious for being willing to eat until they pop, as well as for their ability to steal food from under your nose. Generally all Puggles love their food, so monitoring their daily intake is essential if they are not to become obese.

Crossbreed puppies like the Puggle can look very different from each other, even within the same litter – and from their parents. The Puggle's size, colour, coat type, temperament, energy levels and health risks will vary depending on what traits of the two breeds an individual puppy has inherited from his parents. Puggles range in weight from 15 to 30lb, but one thing to bear in mind is that they often turn out to be larger than people expect.

Generally this crossbreed is chunky, with a short-haired, smooth coat. This is often fawn or black and tan. They have some of the Pug's facial wrinkling as well as the curly tail and relatively short legs. Standing 10 to 15 inches high at the withers (shoulders), they are more akin to the Beagle in size and have the breed's trademark drooping ears.

Puggles have a short coat which is easy to take care of; a weekly brush is usually enough, unless they have been running through or rolling in mud (or something worse, which is not uncommon). The hairs are short, but Puggles are generally fairly consistent shedders.

They require moderate exercise; again, this will vary according to what traits they have inherited and how much exercise they get used to when young. They need at least one daily walk away from the home, preferably more, to satisfy their need to migrate. Given this, they are suitable for apartment life.

Puggles are fairly long lived, with 12 to 14 years being typical, but they can inherit health problems from the Pug or the Beagle. These are cherry eye, epilepsy and hip dysplasia, and some suffer from food and environmental allergies. If you are considering a Puggle, choose one with a longer nose more like the Beagle. Puggles with flatter faces like the Pug, can have breathing problems. One common (non-life threatening) respiratory ailment that Puggles sometimes suffer from is reverse sneezing.

Schnoodle

A Schnoodle is a cross between a Schnauzer and a Poodle. There are three types of Poodle: Standard, Miniature and Toy, and three types of Schnauzer: Giant, Standard and Miniature.

A Schnoodle can be any combination of these, resulting in four types of Schnoodle: Giant, Standard, Miniature and Toy. The most common are the Miniatures - which usually weigh between 10lb and 16lb - however, Giant Schnoodles are also popular.

A Toy Schnoodle is 10 inches or under at the shoulders and under 10lb in weight. This is a cross between a Toy Poodle and a small Miniature Schnauzer. A Giant is a cross between a Standard Poodle and a Giant Schnauzer. A fully grown one will weigh as much as 65 to 80lb and stand 24 to 27 inches high at the shoulders.

Some breeders think the Poodle takes the chunkiness out of the Schnauzer, while the Schnauzer takes the pointed head away from the Poodle. Although there are no written breed characteristics, the Schnoodle should be well-proportioned and athletic with a keen, bold, and lively expression.

Schnoodles are generally F1, or first generation, crosses. In other words, one parent was a Schnauzer and the other was a Poodle. One of the reasons for the Schnoodle's popularity is that both his parents are regarded as hypoallergenic breeds and therefore there's a good chance that the Schnoodle could also be hypoallergenic – although you have to spend time with the puppy to be sure you have no reaction.

The Schnoodle could have a single coat of dense, curly fur like the Poodle, a double coat with a wiry outer coat like the Schnauzer, or a combination of the two. The coat can come in many colours: black, white, grey, apricot, chocolate, black with white markings, wheaten, sable, parti (white with patches of colour) or phantom (black and tan like the Doberman).

Although there is a variety of colours, the Schnoodle coat is almost always curly or at least wavy. As the puppy matures it may develop the rough, wirier hair of the Schnauzer, the softer hair of the Poodle or something in between. Some develop coarser Schnauzer-like hair in places - most notably on the back - with softer Poodle hair on other parts of the body.

One thing that will be almost guaranteed is that the resulting puppy will be low shedding, although you might find the odd fur ball around the house. This is good news to all house-proud owners, but bear in mind that a Schnoodle has to be clipped every eight to 10 weeks and this can cost anything from around £25, or $40, upwards per trim.

There is no defined cut for this crossbreed. Most of them get a general groom - with, perhaps, a #7 shear - with rounded semi-long hair left on the face. Some have a more Terrier-like look with a squarer trim around the face. Owners should check inside their Schnoodle's ears regularly for signs of infection, which both Schnauzers and Poodles are prone to. The area inside the ears is a potential breeding ground for bacteria, and you should ensure it does not become matted with fur, red, hot or smelly. The fur inside the ears should be plucked regularly. If you don't do it, ask your groomer to do it every visit.

Schnoodles' ears are left naturally uncropped. They may have a long ear flap that lays closer to their head and hangs down – like a Poodle - or a shorter ear that stands upright at the base and folds over midway toward the front - like the uncropped ears of a Schnauzer.

The Schnoodle temperament mixes the intellect of the Poodle with the companionship and devotion of the Schnauzer. If treated well when young, Schnoodles make loving, loyal and amusing companions. Being eager to please, they are relatively easy to train. Training should be done in short bursts and efforts should be made to keep it interesting, as it may not be easy to keep their concentration for a long period.

They love playing and distractions. Smaller Schnoodles may be happy as lapdogs; large ones are friskier with higher energy levels and require more time and attention. One of the reasons some Schnoodles end up in rescue shelters is that they have higher energy levels and exercise requirements than their owners realised – particularly large Schnoodles – this can lead to destructive behaviour or excessive barking. Giant Schnoodles are happiest with a couple of hours exercise or more a day.

Schnoodles love to run and jump and require a fair amount of exercise for their size, as well as mental stimulation. They are generally good at canine competitions, being athletic and eager to please. Many love to swim and most love snow.

Schnauzers are affectionate, playful, intelligent and strong-willed, while Poodles are very clever, active and intuitive, and excel in obedience training. Giant Schnauzers can be protective and Miniature Schnauzers can be demanding. Schnoodles may inherit any combination of these attributes, but they are generally very people-orientated dogs which thrive on interaction with their humans. They do not enjoy being left alone for hours on end and can suffer from separation anxiety.

By nature neither of the parent breeds is aggressive with other dogs, and provided a Schnoodle is socialised with other dogs when young – and this is particularly important with Giants – they do well with other canines. Schnoodles are now being used as therapy dogs in hospitals, schools and nursing homes.

The potential Schnoodle health problems are those associated with Poodles and Schnauzers, and include eye issues, (if one of the parents is a Mini Schnauzer, ask to see eye screening certificates), urinary stones, Addison's disease and Cushing's disease. Having said that, Schnoodles are relatively healthy dogs, with the small ones living anywhere from 12 to 16 or 17 years, larger dogs have a shorter lifespan.

Maltipoo

The Maltipoo is a cross between a Toy or Miniature Poodle and a Maltese, a small breed in the Kennel Club's Toy group which is thought to have originated in ancient times on the Mediterranean island of Malta.

The Maltese has had a few different names during its long history; it was known as the ancient dog of Malta, the Roman ladies' dog, the Maltese lion dog and even as "Cokie" in the USA in the 1960s for some inexplicable reason. Its origins have also become blurred in the mists of time, with evidence of the breed being descended either from a Spitz-type dog in Switzerland or the Tibetan Terrier, or a mixture of both.

The Maltese was bred as a companion, although it is a lively little dog for its size, and remains active well into old age. As Poodles are also alert and lively dogs, the Maltipoo is normally jaunty and, like the Maltese, keeps going for years.

These are affectionate dogs which very much love their humans, so are not suitable for leaving at home alone all day as they can suffer from separation anxiety – even to the extent of harming themselves in extreme cases. They are playful dogs which have a sense of fun and love to chase after a ball. Be aware that this little crossbreed does not tolerate very hot or very cold conditions, so exercise should be limited on hot days and a coat may be needed for winter.

Maltipoos are ideally suited to a person who is around all day and who has time to take them out for a daily walk. They can live in an apartment, but are happier in a house with an enclosed garden. If you live in a flat, you might consider a breed or crossbreed with lower natural energy levels. The Maltipoo should get at least 30 minutes of exercise a day – although some of this could be playing in the home or garden.

By temperament, many Maltipoos are what the Brits call feisty and the Americans call spunky. Early socialisation and training is a must to get them used to other dogs and people, although they often do well with other canines. Once trained with positive techniques and rewards, the Maltipoo will love to show off his or her tricks.

The critical age for socialisation is up to 18 or 20 weeks; take the dog everywhere with you. After that the window closes rapidly, which doesn't mean an older dog can't be socialised, it is just more of a challenge as they are less receptive to new things than when young– just like us humans! You CAN teach an old dog new tricks, it just takes longer.

As with all small dogs, the Maltipoo should be treated like a dog, not like a baby. They are happier and more relaxed when assured of their place in the home's pecking order – and that should be below their owners. This crossbreed may not be a good choice if you have very small children, due to its size, delicacy and also the fact that some can be a little intolerant of toddlers. If this is the case, time should be spent training the dog and all time spent with little children should be supervised.

Sadly, research in Australia has shown that the Maltese is the number one dog in rescue shelters there, and the reason is constant barking. Again, early socialisation and plenty of exercise and play is the key. The Maltipoo is undoubtedly cute and cuddly, but don't make the mistake of thinking that he doesn't need exercise or stimulation, because he does. By the way, he barks but will probably welcome strangers with a wagging tail, so he's an excellent watch dog, but no guard dog.

The Maltipoo varies in size from around eight to 14 inches at the withers (shoulders), weighing from five to 20lb. The coat may vary widely from dead straight to wavy or curly and in texture it might be silky like the Maltese or more frizzy or woolly. There are many different colours although, as the Maltese is always white, the most common colours are anything from white to black and every shade in between.

Don't be surprised if your Maltipoo puppy's coat turns much lighter or darker as (s)he grows, this is normal. Regular brushing and trips to the grooming parlour are required with this crossbreed, and cleaning inside the ears to prevent infection should be a part of your grooming regime.

The Maltese and all Poodles are regarded as hypoallergenic breeds, so there is a good chance a Maltese puppy will be low shedding. That does not mean this hybrid is suitable for all allergy sufferers – only time spent with the individual puppy will determine if there is an allergic reaction.

Health problems include Legg-Calve-Perthes disease, luxating patella, PRA (Progressive Retinal Atrophy) and White Shaker Syndrome. Skin problems and allergies can also be an issue with Maltipoos. However, if he remains healthy, this crossbreed stays relatively puppy-like for many years and a typical lifespan is anywhere from 10 to 15 years.

5. Puppies for Allergy Sufferers

Tens of millions of people across the world have allergies. According to the Asthma and Allergy Foundation of America, there are an estimated 50 million sufferers in the USA alone. And one in five of these - 10 million people - are pet allergy sufferers.

Most people think that pet allergies are caused by fur, but that's not true. What they are actually allergic to are proteins – or allergens. These are secreted by the animal's oil glands and then shed with dander, which is dead skin cells. These proteins are also found in dog saliva and urine. So, it is the dander, saliva or urine of a dog which humans normally react to.

Hypoallergenic

It is, however, possible for pet allergy sufferers to enjoy living with a dog without spending all of their time sneezing, wheezing, itching or breaking out in rashes. Millions of people are proving the case - including our family. There are some breeds and crossbreeds which are definitely more suitable for consideration by allergy sufferers. These types of dog are called *'hypoallergenic'*, but what does this mean exactly?

Generally, hypoallergenic dogs are those which do not shed a lot of hair. The official definition of the word hypoallergenic is:

"Having a DECREASED tendency to provoke an allergic reaction."

In other words there is NO CAST IRON GUARANTEE that an allergy sufferer won't have a reaction to a certain type of dog or even an individual dog. But if you do choose a hypoallergenic dog, the chances are greatly reduced. Any dog can cause an allergic reaction, although a low-shedding, hypoallergenic breed such as a Poodle is a much better choice than other shedding breeds, crossbreeds or mixed breeds.

Some breeds of dog, such as Schnauzers, are double coated and the outer coat traps the inner coat and the dander, thereby reducing allergens. Many Australian Labradoodle crossbreeds, for example, have been selectively bred to have a certain type of coat which hardly sheds at all and is often - but by no means always - suitable for people with allergies. From personal experience and numerous comments on our website, it is fair to say that many people who normally suffer from allergies are perfectly fine with hypoallergenic dogs. My partner is allergic to horses, cats and usually dogs, but has no reaction whatsoever to our Miniature Schnauzer, Max. (The good news for dog lovers is that there are more people allergic to cats). However, the other side of the coin is that recue centres are littered with dogs from owners who thought they would not be allergic to their pet – only to get the poor puppy home and find that they couldn't stop sneezing.

But – and this is a very big BUT - it is not simply enough to choose a breed or crossbreed which is hypoallergenic – that is only the first step. Let's clear up a couple of points right away:

- ❖ **No dog is totally non-shedding**
- ❖ **No dog is totally hypoallergenic**

Here are two more very important points:

1. People's pet allergies vary greatly
2. Pet allergy sufferers may react differently to different breeds **as well as individual dogs within that breed.** A sufferer may be fine with one puppy yet have a reaction to another in the same litter

All dogs - even so-called 'hairless' dogs, like the Xoloitzcuintle, or Mexican Hairless dogs pictured here - have hair, dander (dead skin cells, like dandruff), saliva and urine. Therefore all dogs **can** cause allergic reactions. But not all dogs do. Some hypoallergenic dog breeds do not affect pet allergy sufferers as much because of the type or amount of hair that they shed.

Choosing a Puppy

If you have decided to go for a low-shedding, hypoallergenic puppy, then that is just the first step. Your next step is to find a reputable breeder. If you are looking at a pedigree (purebred) dog, a good way of doing this is to check with the Kennel Club in your country by going on to its website and clicking on the breed that you are interested in to find a list of approved or assured breeders. Bear in mind that top breeders often have a waiting list for their pups.

If you are thinking of getting a crossbreed like the Schnoodle (a cross between a Poodle and a Schnauzer), go to Google and type in the name of the crossbreed, followed by the words "breed society."

Although crossbreeds are not registered with the Kennel Clubs, there are organisations which strive to improve the crossbreeds and they have codes of ethics. They also usually have a list of breeders who have agreed to conform to the society's ideals and animal welfare standards.

This is no guarantee of a healthy, hypoallergenic pup, but it is a good starting place, you then have to follow it up with lots of questions – see the section on **Breeders** for what questions to ask.

Mixed breeds are not suitable for people with allergies, as you generally have no idea of the parentage of the dog and it is highly unlikely that all of the pup's ancestors were from the so-called 'non-shedding' breeds. And even if they were, it is still no guarantee. Better to stick with a breed or a crossbreed where you can ask lots of questions of the puppy, its parents and their history.

Once you have found your breeder, DO NOT send money without spending time with a puppy. Indeed, many responsible breeders will not allow this, as they want to be sure their pups are going to good, forever homes and don't want the distressing prospect of having to re-home their puppy because of the owner's allergies. It is upsetting for the family and a disaster for the puppy.

Buying a dog from a breeder with a good reputation is a two-way process. If the breeder isn't asking you any questions – other than how you are going to pay - walk away.

First of all ask if you can visit their adult dogs. Make sure there are no cats around, which could also trigger allergies, and if possible spend time with both parents of any pup you are considering - especially if it's a crossbreed. Within some crossbreeds, like the Labradoodle, some puppies do not shed initially but start to lose hair later as their coat develops.

Choose an experienced breeder with a good track record of breeding low-shedding pups, he or she will have a good idea of how the puppy's coat will develop as the dog grows older.

Four Golden Tips for Allergy Sufferers

❖ **Spend some time alone with the specific pup you are considering** to determine if you have a reaction – and this may be up to two days later. Handle the dog, rub your hands on your face, and lick your hands after you have handled the dog in order to absorb as much potential allergen as you can on your short visit. Allow the pup to lick you – as you may be allergic to his saliva.

❖ **Go back and visit the pup at least once or twice more** before you make that life-changing commitment to buy.

❖ **Take an old towel or piece of cloth and rub the puppy with it**. Take this home with you and handle it to see if you get a delayed reaction.

❖ **Check with the breeder to see if you can return the pup** within a certain time period if you have a reaction to him back at home. But remember that you cannot expect the breeder to take the dog back if the allergies only occur once he has reached adulthood.

Everyone with pet allergies can tolerate a certain amount of allergens (things they are allergic to). If that person is just below his or her tolerance, any additional allergen will push them over the edge, triggering a reaction. So if you reduce the general allergen load in the home, you'll be much more successful when you bring your puppy home.

Top Ten Tips for Reducing Pet Allergens

1. Keep the dog out of your bedroom. We spend around a third of our lives here and keeping animals out can greatly reduce allergic reactions.

2. Do not allow your dog on the couch, bed or any other furniture. Keep him out of the car, or if this is not possible, use car seat covers or a blanket on the seat.

3. Brush your pet regularly - always outdoors - and regularly clean his bedding. Avoid using normal washing powder, as it may trigger a reaction in dogs with sensitive skin.

4. Get a HEPA air cleaner in the bedroom and/or main living room. HEPA stands for High Efficiency Particle Air - a type of air filter that removes 99.97% of all particles.

5. Use a HEPA vacuum cleaner. Neither the HEPA air nor vacuum cleaner is cheap, but if you suffer allergies and really want to share your life and home with a dog, they are worth considering. Both will dramatically improve the quality of the air you breathe in your home.

6. Regardless of what vacuum you use, clean and dust your home regularly.

7. Keep your dog's skin healthy by regularly feeding a good multivitamin and a fatty acid supplement, such as fish oil.

8. Consider using an allergy-reducing spray such as Allerpet, which helps to cleanse the dog's fur of dander, saliva and sebaceous gland secretions. There are also products to reduce allergens from carpets, curtains and furniture.

9. Avoid contact with other dogs and always wash your hands after you have handled any dog, including your own.

10. Consult your doctor and discuss possible immunotherapy or medication. There are medical advances being made in the treatment of

allergies and a range of tablets, sprays and even injections are currently available.

Experts aren't sure whether bathing your dog has any effect on allergy symptoms. Some studies have shown that baths reduce the amount of airborne dander, while others haven't found a difference.

You can certainly try bathing your dog regularly and see what happens; just make sure that it's not the allergy sufferer doing the bathing. Bear in mind that bathing a dog too frequently strips his skin and fur of its natural oils, and always use a medicated shampoo, such as Malaseb, as human shampoos can trigger canine skin problems.

Of course, the only sure-fire way to GUARANTEE no allergic reaction is not to have a dog. But if you have allergies and are determined to go ahead and share your home with Man's Best Friend, then the safest route is to select a 'non-shedding' dog.

The UK and American Kennel Clubs do not make any claims about hypoallergenic dogs or breeds, but they both publish details of **"breeds that generally do well with people with allergies."**

We are not recommending one over another, simply supplying you with the information to make an informed decision.

List of Hypoallergenic Pedigree Dogs

Here is a list of hypoallergenic dogs from both the American Kennel Club (AKC) and The Kennel Club (UK). These are all purebred dogs. While the Kennel Clubs do not guarantee that you will not have an allergic reaction to a particular dog, certain hypoallergenic and non-shedding dog breeds are generally thought to be better for allergy sufferers.

American Kennel Club List

3The American Kennel Club's list of "breeds that generally do well with people with allergies" is:

Bedlington Terrier (pictured
Bichon Frise
Chinese Crested
Irish Water Spaniel
Kerry Blue Terrier
Maltese
Poodle (Toy, Miniature and Standard)
Portuguese Water Dog
Schnauzer (Giant, Standard and Miniature)
Soft Coated Wheaten Terrier
Xoloitzcuintli (FSS Breed)

Kennel Club (UK) List

The KC has this to say about hypoallergenic and non-shedding dog breeds: *"For those owners who wish to obtain a dog which SUPPOSEDLY does not shed its coat, one of these listed breeds may be a suitable choice:"*

Gundog Group
Lagotto Romagnolo
Irish Water Spaniel
Spanish Water Dog (right)

Working Group
Bouvier des Flandres
Giant Schnauzer
Portuguese Water Dog
Russian Black Terrier

Pastoral Group
Hungarian Puli
Komondor

Toy Group
Bichon Frise
Bolognese
Chinese Crested
Coton de Tulear
Havanese
Maltese
Yorkshire Terrier

Utility Group
Lhasa Apso
Intermediate Mexican Hairless
Miniature Mexican Hairless
Standard Mexican Hairless
Miniature Schnauzer
Standard Poodle
Toy Poodle
Miniature Poodle
Shih Tzu
Tibetan Terrier

Terrier Group
Bedlington Terrier
Dandie Dinmont Terrier
Glen of Imaal Terrier
Sealyham Terrier
Soft Coated Wheaten Terrier

Crossbreeds

The Doodle and Poo crossbreeds have become extremely popular over the last few years. All of these are crossed somewhere along the line with a Poodle. Many of these crossbreeds are marketed as suitable for allergy sufferers. Buyer beware, in reality many of them are not. As already discussed, it depends on the individual person's reaction to the individual puppy.

Some people don't want a purebred puppy, they'd rather have a crossbreed, which is the product of crossing two breeds of dog, for example a Cocker Spaniel and a Poodle to create a Cockapoo (pictured, left).

You cannot register a crossbreed with the Kennel Club or get pedigree papers. But despite this, you should always find out about your dog's parents and ancestry – because provided you care for him well, his genes will be the major factor in deciding how healthy he will be.

Just because you get a cross does not mean that the pup will have no health problems. Check what problems the parent breeds are susceptible to and whether health checks have been carried out on the parents and/or pups. Some Poodles, for example, have an inherited disposition to eye, hip or epilepsy problems. Ask to see health certificates.

Although you will not be able to enter your Doodle or Poo in a conformation class run under Kennel Club rules, there are plenty other shows and activities to enjoy with a crossbreed. Agility shows and flyball are becoming increasingly popular, as well as local dog shows. Some are also used as therapy or assistance dogs.

If a crossbreed is for you, then you need to understand the complicated subject of F numbers - or at least have a vague idea what breeders are talking about. F stands for filial when describing cross bred dogs and it comes from the Latin *filius* (son) and means "relating to a son or daughter."

An **F1** Doodle or Poo is a first generation cross. So, with Labradoodles for example, one parent was a Labrador and the other was a Poodle. An F1 Labradoodle is more likely to shed hair than higher generation Labradoodles, as half of its genes are coming from the Labrador, which moults. According to an unofficial Doodle database involving 237 dogs, over half of the F1 Labradoodles shed some hair– although many were light shedders and some caused no reported problems with the allergy sufferers they were living with.

Canine experts believe that a first generation (F1) cross may benefit from 'hybrid vigour.' This is the belief that the first cross between two unrelated purebred lines is healthier and grows better than either parent line. The next generations are worked out by always **adding one number up from the lowest number parent**, and it is thought that hybrid vigour is lost with each successive generation. See **Chapter 4 Crossbreeds** for more information.

❖ An **F2** could be the offspring of two x F1 Labradoodles or the product of an F1 crossed with an F2, F3 or F4 dog.

❖ An **F3** is the offspring of one F2 parent where the other was F2 or higher, for example F2xF3 or F2xF4, etc.

❖ Then you can get an **F1B, F2B, F3B** and so on. The B stands for Backcross. This occurs when a litter has been produced as a result of a backcross to a purebred dog – normally a Poodle. This is usually done to improve consistency of appearance and coat type, often to increase the possibility of a low shedding coat. It is not common practice for breeders to backcross to a Labrador, so a typical F1B might be one quarter Labrador and three quarters Poodle.

A second generation backcross pup **(F2B)** is the result of an F1 bred to a backcross (F1B). Although three generations in the making, F2Bs are technically second generation dogs.

A **multigen** (or **multigeneration**) crossbreed is the result of successive breeding of crossbreed to crossbreed – such as Cockapoo to Cockapoo, Goldendoodle to Goldendoodle or Labradoodle to Labradoodle) - rather than mating a pedigree dog with another pedigree dog. While hybrid vigour may be lost, the advantage of multigeneration puppies is that good breeders can reproduce a more consistent size, appearance and coat type. (Pictured is a Cavapoo).

So, although a multigen is not a purebred, where prospective owners have a pretty definite idea of what the adult dog will look like, they have a better idea than with an F1 puppy, which could take after the Poodle or the other breed.

By the way, all Australian Labradoodles are multigeneration, but not all multigenerations are Australian Labradoodles. Because multigens have become very popular - and expensive with prices sometimes rising to four or even five figures - there are people who advertise multigens and charge a high price for puppies which are either not technically multigeneration or are not the product of careful breeding. See **Chapter 6. Choosing a Good Breeder** for more information.

Poodles have a wool-type coat, so breeding from Poodles increases the likelihood of the offspring having a low-shed or non-shedding coat. It also introduces popular new colours such as red and parti (white and another colour).

There are so many new "designer" crossbreeds springing up all the time. Here is a list of popular ones below, with a star by the name if both parent breeds are regarded as hypoallergenic.

Affenpoo - Affenpinscher x Poodle

Airedoodle - Airedale Terrier x Poodle

Aki-Poo - Akita x Poodle

Australian Labradoodle – a multigeneration Labradoodle

Bassetoodle - Basset Hound x Poodle

Bichpoo * - Bichon Frise x Poodle

Bordoodle - Border Collie x Poodle

Cadoodle - Collie x Poodle

Cavapoo - Cavalier King Charles Spaniel x Poodle

Chipoo - Chihuahua x Poodle

Cockapoo (Cockerpoo) - Cocker Spaniel x Poodle

Doxiepoo -Dachshund x Poodle

English Boodle – Bulldog x Poodle

Foodle - Fox Terrier x Poodle

Goldador –Golden Retriever x Labrador

Goldendoodle – Golden Retriever x Poodle

Havapoo * – Havanese and Poodle

Irish Doodle - Irish Setter x Poodle

Lhasapoo * - Lhasa Apso x Poodle

Maltipoo * - Maltese x Poodle

Maltese Shih Tzu (Malshi) * - Maltese x Shih Tzu

Papipoo - Papillon x Poodle

Pekepoo (or Peekapoo) - Pekingese x Poodle

Pugapoo – Pug x Poodle

Puggle – Pug x Beagle

Shepadoodle – German Shepherd x Poodle

Shihpoo * – Shih Tzu x Poodle

Schnoodle * – one of the three Schnauzers x Poodle

Springerdoodle – English Springer Spaniel x Poodle

Yorkipoo * – Yorkshire Terrier x Poodle

Zuchon * –*Shih Tzu x Bichon* Frise

No breeder can guarantee that a specific crossbreed (or pedigree dog) will be 100% suitable for an individual allergy sufferer. However, when responsible breeders of crossbreeds select their dams and sires, coat is often an important factor. There is plenty of anecdotal evidence that many of these dogs shed little or no hair and do not trigger a reaction with some allergy sufferers. But each individual case is different; there are no guarantees.

For those people with consistent or severe allergies, another option is to consider a purebred hypoallergenic breed and then follow our guidance to select a breeder and then a puppy. Choosing a suitable dog is not completely straightforward and you do have to put in extra time to ensure you pick the right dog and maybe make a few adjustments at home as well. Remember:

- ❖ No breed or crossbreed is totally non-shedding
- ❖ No breed or crossbreed is totally hypoallergenic

Useful Websites

www.thekennelclub.org.uk The Kennel Club UK

www.akc.org American Kennel Club

www.akcreunite.org Helps find lost or stolen dogs in USA, register your puppy's microchip

www.ukcdogs.com United Kennel Club (North America)

www.ckc.ca Canadian Kennel Club

www.apdt.com Association of Pet Dog Trainers USA

www.cappdt.ca Canadian Association of Professional Pet Dog Trainers

www.apdt.co.uk Association of Pet Dog Trainers UK

www.dogfoodadvisor.com Useful unbiased information on grain-free and hypoallergenic dog foods

www.dogstrust.org.uk – rehomes dogs across the UK

www.battersea.org.uk Battersea Dogs Homers, London

www.petfinder.com/animal-shelters-and-rescues/search List of dog rescue centres in the USA by state

Pet insurance USA www.consumersadvocate.org/pet-insurance/best-pet-insurance.html

Pet insurance UK www.which.co.uk/money/insurance/reviews-ns/pet-insurance

Disclaimer

This book has been written to provide helpful information on dogs. It is not meant to be used, nor should it be used, to diagnose or treat any medical condition. For diagnosis or treatment of any animal medical problem, consult a qualified veterinarian. The author is not responsible for any specific health or allergy conditions that may require medical supervision and is not liable for any damages or negative consequences from any treatment, action, application or preparation, to any person reading or following the information in this book. References are provided for informational purposes only and do not constitute endorsement of any websites or other sources.

WHICH DOG BREED? - The Insider's Guide

© Copyright 2014-2015 Linda Whitwam

This book is an excerpt from the in-depth Canine Handbook manual **How to Pick the Perfect Puppy.**

Once you have chosen the type of dog you want, **How to Pick the Perfect Puppy** outlines in detail how to go on and find the right breeder and then choose the individual puppy most likely to have the temperament and energy levels to fit in with you and your family.

 It also covers bringing a puppy home, caring for a puppy, understanding your puppy's mind, obedience training, housetraining and crate training.

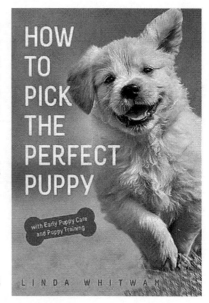

USA: www.amazon.com/How-Pick-The-Perfect-Puppy/dp/1500423467

UK: www.amazon.co.uk/How-Pick-The-Perfect-Puppy/dp/1500423467

READERS' OFFER

If you have purchased **Which Dog Breed** and go on to purchase **How to Pick the Perfect Puppy,** leave a review of either book on Amazon and send the link with your review to thehandbooks@btinternet.com and we will refund the cost of **Which Dog Breed** with an Amazon voucher.

 If you love dogs and would like to learn more, follow us on Twitter **@CanineHandbooks**

12525733R00068

Printed in Great Britain
by Amazon